ELITE SERIES

EDITOR: MARTIN WINDROW

The US Marine Corps since 1945

Text by LEE E. RUSSELL

Colour plates by ANDY CARROLL

OSPREY PUBLISHING LONDON

Published in 1984 by
Osprey Publishing Ltd
Member company of the George Philip Group
12–14 Long Acre, London WC2E 9LP
© Copyright 1984 Osprey Publishing Ltd

British Library Cataloguing in Publication Data

Russell, Lee E.
  The US Marine Corps since 1945.—(Osprey
  Elite series; 2)
  1. United States. *Marine Corps*
  —History
  I. Title
  359.9'6'0973 VE 23

  ISBN 0-85045-574-X

Filmset in Great Britain
Printed in Hong Kong

Acknowledgments
The author wishes to thank the following for their assistance in the preparation of this book:

The personnel of the Marine Corps Public Affairs Office in New York City, most especially, Gy. Sgt. Randy Bare and Gy. Sgt. William V. Brown; MSgt. Wyatt of the 2nd MARDIV-PAO, Camp Lejeune; SSgt. Fitzgerald of the Mobility and Logistics Division, Quantico; Mr. K. L. Smith-Christmas, Curator of Material History, and Mr. Dan Crawford, Reference Section, Marine Corps Museum, Washington DC; Col. John Greenwood and MSgt. Joseph D. Dodd, of the Marine Corps Association and *Leatherneck* Magazine; the personnel of the Marine Corps Uniform Board, Headquarters, Marine Corps, Washington DC; Mr. Frank Kerr of the Chosin Reservoir Veteran's Association, 'The Chosin Few'; and special thanks to Mr. Severino Mendez, and to the following 'Post '45' Marines: Chris DiAngelo, Michael Pahios, John Olsen, Charles 'Chuck' Haig, Paul R. Piazza, Dorothy Kretci Colletti, Lt. Col. Harry T. Milne(Ret.) and Maj. Paul E. Sanders(Ret.), for their help. All opinions and conclusions are, however, the author's own.

The US Marine Corps since 1945

The Post-War Marines

The US Marine Corps, the oldest of America's armed forces, was established on 10 November 1775. It became part of the permanent establishment by Act of Congress on 11 July 1798. The next day, President John Adams appointed William Ward Burrows as its first Commandant. In the 19th century the Corps' name became synonymous with romantic adventures and exotic foreign landscapes. In World War I, Marines served prominently in France, and in World War II they fought against Japan in the Pacific on land and sea and in the air. By 1945, the Corps had established itself in two chosen rôles: as an intervention force, ready to guarantee American lives and interests around the world; and as the leading exponent of combined amphibious operations against hostile shores. The next 40 years would see much use of these talents in two major wars and a dozen smaller crises. In the meantime the Corps would survive major inter-service disputes and some internal problems of its own. The story begins in August 1945, with the dropping of the atomic bomb and the surrender of Japan.

* * *

The end of World War II found the US Marine Corps at its peak strength of 473,000. Its combat elements, comprising two Corps, six Divisions and five Marine Air Wings, were completely deployed against Japan. In the midst of preparations for the invasion of Japan, the atomic bomb came as a total surprise. The new weapon would shortly have major implications for the Corps, but for the moment it was the enemy's sudden surrender that occupied their attention. On 30 August 1945, elements of 2/4 Marines (2nd Battalion, 4th Marine Regiment) from the 6th Marine Division carried out the first landings in Japan. Along with Army Airborne troops, their mission was to secure

Marine Recruiting Sergeants model the new (left) and old (right) versions of the enlisted Blue Dress uniform, January 1947. At that time the Recruiting Service shoulder patch and 1937 chevrons were still authorised, but both would disappear by the end of that year. (USMC 404324)

military facilities in the Tokyo area for the arrival of Gen. Douglas MacArthur. The choice of the 4th Marines was deliberate. The regiment had been formed in 1944, from veteran Raider units: the original 4th had surrendered in the Philippines, in the dark days of 1942. In mid-September 1945 further units arrived, this time from the 2nd and 5th Divisions.

Despite some initial apprehension, the Japanese proved as submissive in defeat as they were implacable in war, and the duties of the occupation

Retirement ceremony for Secretary of the Navy John M. Chafee in 1972. The Honor Guard wear the special ceremonial Blue-White Dress, with MI rifles and white bayonet scabbards; the officer's Sam Browne is worn with this uniform only. (USMC A702747)

forces consisted mostly of the supervised destruction of war material. Another task was the repatriation of Allied prisoners of war, many of whom had suffered years of captivity.

While the 2nd and 5th Divisions disarmed bypassed Japanese island garrisons, other Marines of the 1st and 6th Divisions were sent to China to accept the surrender of Japanese troops stationed there. They landed in late September and early October, and moved to Tientsin and Tsingtao by rail. The Japanese proved the least of their problems, as northern China was torn by disorder and revolution. As they secured railroads and communications, the Marines quickly became embroiled. They would remain so for nearly three years, and suffer casualties both dead and wounded. Although organised Red Chinese forces left them alone, they quickly became targets for every bandit

and Red guerilla in northern China. The last Marine forces were not to depart until June 1949.

Aside from the units involved in occupation duties, the rest of the Marine Corps was concerned with a contradictory task. With the war over, there was a public outcry for speedy demobilisation. The 3rd, 4th and 5th Divisions were returned to the United States in late 1945 and early 1946, and the 2nd followed in June. After out-processing returnees, the skeleton 2nd Division was moved to Camp Lejeune, North Carolina, to become part of the peacetime establishment. The 3rd, 4th and 5th were decommissioned. In early 1946 the bulk of Marine occupation troops in Japan departed for China, and in May Marine responsibilities there were consolidated under the 1st Division. The 6th then departed in its turn for the States and decommissioning. By the end of 1946 the Corps' strength had shrunk to less than 100,000.

As this was accomplished, the Marines turned their attention to the tactical problems created by atomic weapons. A new amphibious doctrine was created, under which aircraft carriers would take the place of transports, and helicopters that of landing craft. At the time, it should be remembered, the Marines had only a handful of helicopters, and the largest held three people including the pilot. It was a revolutionary doctrine, and the Corps even managed to divert some of its limited resources to tests in exercises in the late 1940s.

'The Right to Fight'—the Unification Controversy

The ships and helicopters themselves would have to wait. The Truman years were hard times for the military. Post-war budget cuts were only the beginning. After the war a series of proposals were made to reform the American defence establishment. Now chiefly remembered for the B-36 controversy and the establishment of the Air Force as a separate service, the unification issue also had serious implications for the Marine Corps. Between 1946 and 1950 the Corps was faced with no less than three attempts to change its rôle and status within the military: taken together, they constituted a direct attempt to legislate the Marines out of existence.

The first two attempts, in mid-1946 and 1947, concerned changes in the status of the Fleet Marine Force (FMF)—the command under which Marine combat forces operate. To understand this properly, it is important to appreciate the particular status of the Marine Corps. While traditionally operating alongside the Navy, with its personnel often under Navy control, the Marines are still a separate branch of the Armed Forces, established by Congress, with their own missions. Legally, the Navy and Marine Corps are separate services reporting to the same civilian chief, the Secretary of the Navy.

During World War II, to simplify command procedures, the Marines placed all their FMF forces (their combat Divisions and Air Wings) under Navy control. After the war the Navy wished to formalise this arrangement. In 1946 a bill to that effect—S.2044—was introduced in Congress. Its practical effect was to reduce the Marine Corps to the status of a Navy branch, 'like the Bureau of Yards and Docks', as Marine Commandant Alexander Vandegrift indignantly phrased it.

Vandegrift, his Medal of Honor from Guadal-

The Officer's White Summer Dress, worn here at a Washington retirement ceremony in 1973. (USMC A704515)

canal hanging at his throat, made an impassioned speech before Congress in May 1946. It saved the day temporarily; but the same bill was back a year later. This time it was accompanied by a directive prohibiting comment by any serving officer! In response, Marine Brig. Gen. Merritt A. 'Red Mike' Edson resigned his commission, and made the rounds of Capitol Hill as a civilian. At the sacrifice of his career, Edson achieved his goal. The National Security Act of 1947 confirmed the Marines' status and mission within the new Department of Defense.

The third crisis was more serious: the political lobbying on the Marines' behalf had aroused annoyance in high places. The National Defense Act had opened a debate on the future size and structure of the Armed Forces, and serious changes were being discussed. Vandegrift retired in December 1947, and was replaced by Gen. Clifton B. Cates. In March 1948 President Truman, himself an ex-Army officer with little love for the naval services, appointed an old political crony, Louis Johnson, as the new Secretary of Defense.

Johnson, after obtaining a pliable Secretary of the Navy, set about a major budget reduction for the Marine Corps. The Corps was reduced to 70,000 effectives, and the Marines were forced to disband service troops to keep alive their two-division peacetime structure. Thwarted in his intent, Johnson ordered the Corps the following year to disband specific units, cutting their strength to only ten under-strength battalions. His office refused to recognise the two-division structure, and he publicly announced his intention to reduce the Corps still further. Eventually it would comprise a handful of units, none above a battalion in size. In a fit of pettiness, he forbade the Marines to celebrate the Corps' Official Birthday, 10 November; confiscated Gen. Cates's official car; and reduced the ceremonial honours to which he was entitled. More importantly, he publicly discussed merging the Marine Corps with the Army, a project in which the Army also took a malicious interest.

Johnson overstepped himself with his pronouncements, and Congressional leaders forced him to retract his public statements. The Birthday, car and honours were restored, but Johnson's intent never wavered. In June 1950 he announced a further Corps reduction to only six battalions in fiscal year 1951. It was not to be. By November, Johnson himself was gone and the Corps was rapidly expanding. On 25 June 1950 the North Korean People's Army had invaded South Korea. America was once more at war, and had need of her Marines.

A Brigade for Korea

The invasion took official Washington by surprise. So did the collapse of the South Korean Army, under attack by veteran troops and Russian-made T-34 tanks. Seoul fell on 27 June. By chance, the Russians were boycotting the Security Council of the United Nations that month, and the Secretary-General was able to call an emergency session. The United Nations called on North Korea to cease its aggression, and requested member nations to render aid to South Korea. The United States was the first to respond.

Originally it was hoped that US airpower, based in Japan, would make a difference. It did not. The decision was made to commit US ground troops, and some small Army units were airlifted in from Japan. These were occupation troops, and their training and equipment were deficient: the NKPA brushed them aside and hurried south. More Army troops were sent, but there was a limit to what was available. The US had not planned to fight a conventional war, and was sadly short of combat troops. It was in this atmosphere that the Joint Chiefs of Staff, of which Marine Commandant Cates was not a member, met in early July. Due to the seriousness of the crisis, he was allowed to sit in, and his offer of a Marine Air-Ground Brigade was accepted.

On 7 July, the 1st Provisional Marine Brigade was stripped out of the skeleton 1st Division at Camp Pendleton, California. Its depleted ranks augmented by drafts from other units, the brigade sailed from San Diego on 12 July, 6,500 strong. It comprised the 5th Marine Regiment (Lt. Col. Raymond L. Murray) and Marine Air Group 33—MAG-33—(Brig. Gen. Thomas H. Cushman). The

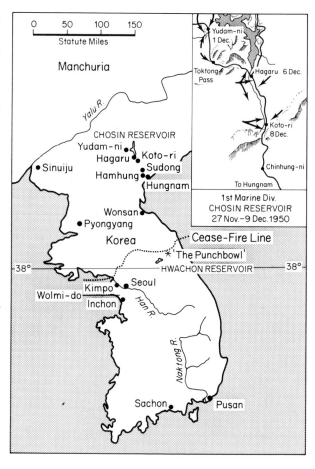

6

Air Group had three fighter-bomber squadrons of F4U Corsairs, and one of light observation planes. Four Sikorsky HO3S-1 helicopters were hastily added, out of a handful in service. The brigade commander was Brig. Gen. Edward A. Craig.

Meanwhile, on 10 July, Lt. Gen. Lemuel Shepherd, commander of the FMF–Pacific, arrived in Tokyo to confer with General MacArthur, the Commander-in-Chief, Far East. MacArthur pointed to a wall map of Korea and remarked: 'If I only had the 1st Marine Division under my command again, I would land them here . . .' The stem of his

Posed against an amtrack in late autumn 1950, San Francisco Marine Reservists serving in Korea display a range of combat dress. Seen here are M1941 and M1943 Field Jackets; utility uniforms worn over sweaters; and (top left) the Tanker's Jacket issued only to Marine tank crews. Note brown leather gloves and OD wool 'inserts'. (USMC A5536)

Veterans of the Chosin fighting withdrawn to reserve in January 1951 wearing a variety of upper garments, with M1942 utility trousers and a mixture of utility and pile caps. Left to right: M1944 utility jacket, Marine pile-lined vest, M1942 utility jacket, Army HBT jacket, Marine tan-khaki shirt. (USMC A5934)

Men of Co.B, 1/5 Marines pause on a Naktong hillside for a radio check in August 1950. They wear a mixture of M1942 and M1944 utilities with leggings. The World War II-vintage radios are (centre) the SCR-536 'handie-talkie', and (right) the SCR-300 'walkie-talkie'—the nickname often wrongly used for the former set. (USMC A2142)

corncob pipe indicated the port of Inchon. Shepherd assured him he could have the division by September if he requested it. MacArthur did so immediately.

The brigade arrived at Pusan on 2 August 1950. By this time, three under-strength Army divisions and what was left of the ROK (Republic of Korea) army had stabilised the front along the Naktong River around the port of Pusan. The situation was precarious, however, and for the next month the Marines would be used as a mobile reserve—a 'fire brigade' to contain any NKPA breakthroughs. They went into action for the first time on 7 August, the eighth anniversary of the landing on Guadalcanal. They spearheaded an attack at Sachon, to redress a threat to the extreme south of the perimeter. With the support of MAG-33's two Corsair squadrons, flying from escort carriers (the 5th Air Force in Japan had commandeered the third for night intruder missions), the Marines pushed the enemy back.

On 13 August the Marines were suddenly pulled out and rushed north to Obong-ni, where the NKPA's 4th Division was across the Naktong and threatening Miryang. The objective was a terrain feature called 'No Name Ridge', and the 5th attacked in column of battalions on the morning of 17 August. On the fourth try they reached the crest. That night the NKPA counter-attacked, but were driven off. At dawn, calling down air strikes directly in front of their positions, 1/5 pushed over the top and the NKPA fled in panic toward the river. MAG-33 cut them off and chopped them down. Twelve hundred dead and most of the Communist division's equipment were left on the battlefield. The NKPA 4th was finished as a fighting unit, but the cost had been high: 2/5 in particular had been badly hurt.

The NKPA was back in September, in an all-out effort to break through the perimeter at every point. In the north the NKPA 9th Division broke through the newly arrived US Army 2nd Division and once more threatened Miryang. The threat was judged most critical in this sector, and the Marine Brigade was ordered to return to its old battlefield. On 3 September, together with Army troops, the Marines attacked. In a day of heavy fighting the enemy was pushed back. On 5 September the brigade went into reserve to load-out for Inchon.

Inchon and Seoul

Meanwhile, the Corps was coping with bringing the rest of the 1st Division to war strength. The 70,000-man Corps, with worldwide commitments, was already over-extended. Fortunately, there was one ready source of manpower. On 19 July 1950 the Corps called 33,500 Marine Reservists to the colours, many of them veterans of World War II. The 2nd Division at Lejeune contributed the bulk of its personnel as cadre for the 1st Regiment at Pendleton. Its own 6th Marines were re-designated the 7th Regiment, and left directly for Korea. Even the 6th Fleet in the Mediterranean gave up its Battalion Landing Team (BLT), which headed east via Suez and Singapore.

Maj. Gen. Oliver P. Smith, the new commander of the 1st Division, arrived in Tokyo on 22 August. Because of tidal fluctuations, the Inchon landings would have to take place on 15 September. There were 24 days to prepare. The operation itself was a major gamble. The tides were treacherous and the approach difficult. There were no proper beaches, and the landings would be made against a seawall. Worse, American amphibious forces were a rusty travesty of their wartime might. Only the rashness of the operation recommended it: that, and the hope that success would cut the NKPA off from its supply lines, liberate Seoul, and turn the war around.

After preliminary bombardments, 3/5 Marines landed at dawn on 15 September to secure two harbour islands, Wolmi-do and Suwolmi-do. The rest of the force went in with the next favourable tide, at dusk. The landings went off perfectly. From his flagship, Gen. MacArthur sent congratulations: 'The Navy and the Marines have never shone more brightly than this morning'.

On the morning of the 16th the division moved out. Kimpo airport fell on the 17th. The same day, two battalions of the 5th crossed the Han River in amtracks (amphibious tractors) supported by naval gunfire. After heavy fighting, they secured the high ground north of Seoul.

On 24 September the 1st and 5th Marines entered the city itself. The NKPA resisted stubbornly. They held Seoul in strength, and had to

Camouflage clothing saw very limited use in Korea but these Marines photographed in 1952 have acquired sets of M1944 pattern; note that they are worn *over* the M1951 Armor Vest. The cylindrical objects on their belts are M15 White Phosphorus smoke grenades, grey with yellow markings. (USMC A163258)

be rooted out in three days of street fighting. The city was declared secure on the 27th. In the south, the US 8th Army broke out of the Pusan perimeter and pushed north. The NKPA, cut off from supplies and bled white on the Naktong, fled before them in disorder. The war seemed suddenly won. The United Nations decided to continue the war into North Korea. In early October the Marines returned to Inchon to re-embark.

The Chosin Reservoir

The next operation was an administrative landing at Wonsan, on the opposite side of the peninsula. There was a week's delay as the harbour was cleared of mines. To their embarrassment, the Marines were greeted on landing by comedian Bob Hope and a USO troupe. The city had been captured from the land side; but elements of the 1st Marines were needed for local clearing operations, which lasted until early November. For geographic reasons, operations on the east coast were being conducted by X Corps independent of the 8th Army. The 5th and 7th Marines were ordered to advance north from Hamhung to the Yalu River and the Chinese border. Their first objective was the Chosin Reservoir.

In Tokyo they were saying that the war would be

Koto-ri, December 1950: two views of machine gun troops during the Chosin campaign, sheltering behind a railway embankment and barricades of field packs—the ground was frozen too hard to dig in. Note that these support troops carry M1 carbines, and even the old 1903 Springfield bolt-action rifle. (USMC A5432, A5434)

over by Christmas; at the front Gen. Smith wasn't so sure. His division was dangerously over-extended along the single narrow road which connected him to the rear.

Smith's apprehensions were realised on 2 November, when advancing elements of the 7th Marines made heavy contact with Chinese forces north of Hamhung. The Chinese, roughly handled, broke contact four days later and seemingly disappeared. The Marines advanced once more;

but to add to Smith's worries, winter had come to North Korea. Temperatures sank to an Arctic −35°F at night, and rarely rose above 0°F in daytime. The cold froze rations, morphine, and the perspiration inside rubber shoepacs. Vehicles broke down, shells did not explode, and automatic weapons refused to fire. It was impossible to dig into the frozen earth without explosives. Only two events gave Smith cheer. One was the arrival of the 1st Marine Air Wing (Maj. Gen. Field Harris), with MAG-12 and three more Corsair squadrons. The other was the arrival of welcome British reinforcements in the shape of 41 Commando, Royal Marines.

On 24 November Smith was reluctantly preparing for an offensive ordered by X Corps. It would coincide with one in the west, where 80 miles of mountains separated the Marines from 8th Army. On the 25th, 8th Army was heavily attacked, but the orders still stood. The two Marine regiments concentrated at Yudam-ni dutifully jumped off on the 27th, only to be stopped cold by the Chinese. Unknown to X Corps, eight Chinese divisions had been concentrated against the Marines. That night, they struck. At the time, the Marines were deployed as follows.

Furthest north, at Yudam-ni west of the reservoir, were the 5th and 7th Marines, with most of the divisional artillery (three battalions of the 11th Marines). Next south, the Toktong Pass was secured by F Company, 2/7. Hagaru-ri, site of Smith's headquarters and an unfinished airfield, was held by one under-strength battalion, the 3/1 Marines, with some engineers and miscellaneous support troops. Koto-ri was defended by 2/1 and the 1st Regiment's headquarters. The 1st's commander was the legendary Col. Lewis 'Chesty' Puller, already the most decorated Marine in the Corps' long history. Also present was 41 Commando, under Lt. Col. Douglas Drysdale, and the rest of 3/1. Furthest south, 1/1 secured the Funchilin Pass at Chinhung-ni.

From north to south, the Marines were stretched out 70 miles along a single road. On the first night, 27/28 November 1950, the Chinese attacked every garrison from Yudam-ni to Koto-ri and cut the road in dozens of places. Three Army battalions east of the reservoir (eventually known as Task Force Faith after their final commander) were also

Marine machine gunners and BAR men test the new M1951 Winter Clothing in Korea. The BAR-man's M1937 Magazine Belt hangs unfastened. (USMC A158139)

attacked. The situation was perilous in the extreme. Smith's solution was simple, but grim. All the garrisons would have to stand firm until the main force could fight its way down to relieve them. The situation was worst at Hagaru. Two Chinese divisions had nearly taken it the first night. Smith ordered Puller, himself holding off a division at Koto, to send a relief force north.

Puller chose 41 Commando, 30 tanks, and the orphan company of 3/1 to make the effort. Under Lt. Col. Drysdale's command, they struggled north all day on the 29th, with their flanks covered by Marine aircraft, but delayed by numerous roadblocks. At nightfall a huge Chinese ambush tore the column to pieces. Drysdale, wounded, but true to his orders, fought his way into Hagaru near midnight. He brought a dozen tanks and 300 men to help save the garrison the next night, but most of his command had been destroyed on the road.

Yudam-ni to Hagaru

At Yudam-ni the regimental commanders (Murray, 5th, and Col. H. L. Litzenberg, 7th) were facing several problems. On 28 November they had been attacked by three divisions of the IX Chinese Field Army. While still defending against this threat, they would have to execute a motor march south, fighting their way along the blocked road.

HRS-1 helicopter crews of HMR-161, the first USMC helicopter squadron to reach Korea, wear the basic Mk.II Life Preserver over standard utilities. Note rank bars and Corps badge worn on front of cap, right. (USMC A132519)

First, however, Litzenberg ordered 1/7 (Lt. Col. Raymond Davis) to advance overland and relieve the beleaguered company at the Toktong Pass, under heavy attack since the 28th.

On 1 December Davis broke out of the perimeter and led his men into the mountains. Already exhausted by five days of combat, they found the eight-mile forced march in temperatures as low as −24°F a nightmare: two of Davis's men went insane. At dawn he linked up with the isolated F Co., 2/7. In an epic defence, Fox Company had held for five days against two Chinese regiments. Only 82 men out of 240 were still alive and unwounded; but they still had their hill. On 3 December the vanguard of the 5th Marines reached the pass by road, and the long column passed slowly through.

On the night of 30 November, the Chinese attacked Hagaru again in divisional strength. At one point the perimeter was breached and the attackers reached the unfinished airstrip. Combat engineers of the 1st Marine Engineer Battalion counter-attacked. Fighting hand-to-hand under brilliant electric floodlights, they drove the Chinese back, then resumed work once more.

At dawn on the 1st the Army Task Force east of the reservoir attempted to march the 12 miles to Hagaru, covered by Marine aircraft. Burdened by casualties, they were four miles short of their goal at dusk, when Col. Faith was killed. His command fell apart in a massive ambush, and only a few hundred stragglers reached safety. The next morning the Marines mounted a rescue expedition to the site.

They found some 300 Army wounded abandoned on the ice, left as bait by the Chinese in hopes of destroying a rescue force. Marine Corsairs put an end to this plan, and under their protection the wounded were gathered and returned to Hagaru.

The main column from the north reached Hagaru-ri by the evening of the 3rd. Brave men wept as they marched in. Smith wrote: 'The critical part of the operation had been completed.' The airfield was now operational, and on the morning of the 4th the first transport 'planes arrived to fly out the wounded—over 4,000 in three days. Smith also took the opportunity to correct what he felt was a misapprehension. In response to Press reports that the Marines were retreating for the first time in their 175-year history, he stated: 'Gentlemen, we are not retreating. We are merely attacking in another direction'. As good as his word, he refused an Air Force offer to evacuate his division by air, and instead had 500 replacements flown in for his rifle companies. The column rested until the 6th and then moved out: the 7th Marines in the lead, the 5th acting as rearguard.

Hagaru to the sea

On the march to Koto-ri, the Marines would rely on the same tactics that had got them safely to Hagaru. Every officer and man who could walk would march. While the point of the column advanced, rifle battalions would climb adjacent hills to secure the road. Flanks and reverse slopes would be left to 1st MAW's Corsairs and Navy planes from four fast carriers of TF 77. The first obstacle south of Hagaru was East Hill, which the Chinese had held since the first night, defying every effort to dislodge them. With the aid of 76 Corsair missions, the hill was cleared. That night, 1/5 and 2/5 stood off a division-size attack on the rearguard, and a second effort against the convoy was beaten off by clerks, truck drivers and artillerymen. The next day was spent pushing through roadblocks set up amid the wrecked vehicles of Task Force Drysdale. By nightfall on 7 December the division reached Koto-ri.

While the worst of the ordeal was behind them, two obstacles still remained south of Koto. The first was a bridge which the Chinese had blown at the Funchilin Pass. The second was Hill 1081, which dominated the defile at just that point. Smith ordered the 7th Marines to attack south on 8 December, and 1/1 to move north against the hill overland from the rear. Both units moved out in a blinding snowstorm on the coldest day yet. As the men of 1/1 struggled over icy, rugged hills, the 7th could make little progress against the strongly held position: after two weeks of unrelenting combat, some of its battalions were down to 130 men. On 9 December 1/1 took the Chinese by surprise from the rear, stormed the hill and killed its defenders to the last man. With the hill in American hands, Smith requested an airdrop of eight sections of a Treadway bridge. This was accomplished by Air Force 'planes from Japan; and the road was at last open. On 12 December the 1st Marine Division marched into Hungnam. They had come out tired, but proud and intact, bringing their wounded and most of the dead, along with vehicles, weapons and prisoners. In the process they had destroyed six

M26 Pershings of Co.A, 1st Marine Tank Bn. approach Wolmi-Do's Green Beach on the morning of 15 September 1950, in the course of the Inchon landings. They were to be in combat within minutes of landing, in support of 'Item' Co., 3/5 Marines.

Chinese divisions and inflicted approximately 37,500 casualties on the enemy, including at least 25,000 dead. Unmolested, the Marines loaded onto transports and departed from Hungnam with the rest of X Corps on 15 December.

The Chosin campaign had been a supreme test of

Men of 1/7 Marines clamber on to an M46 Patton of 1st Marine Tank Bn. during training: Korea, June 1952. Note rear view of Marine M1951 Armor Vest, World War II-issue camouflage helmet covers, and leggings; the sergeant (left) has inked chevrons on his utility sleeve. (USMC A162772)

A 'Stateside' Marine fighter pilot in the early 1950s, wearing A-10A Khaki Summer Flying Helmet with boom mike attachment; A-14 Demand Oxygen Mask; and B-8 Goggles. With his Z-1 Flying Coveralls he wears a Mk.II Life Preserver, low brown shoes, B-3 Flying Gloves, and a commercial knife. (USMC 31371)

courage and discipline for all involved. Nevertheless, it would have been a failure except for 1st MAW. Over 3,700 sorties had been flown in support of the division. Gen. Smith wrote to its commander, in heartfelt appreciation: 'During the long reaches of the night and in the snowstorms, many a Marine prayed for the coming of day or clearing weather when he knew he would again hear the welcome roar of your planes. . .'. Gen.

Harris's pride and satisfaction were tempered with sorrow: his officer son had been killed in action on the march to Koto-ri.

The division arrived at Pusan amid rumours that it would be sent to Indo-China to help the French. That rumour was a decade premature; instead the 1st passed into 8th Army reserve for a quiet month's rest, followed by a month of fighting guerillas along the east coast.

Korea 1951–53

In February and March 1951, the Marines participated in two limited UN offensives, code-named 'Killer' and 'Ripper', which restored the front above the 38th Parallel. The Marines were holding a sector near the Hwachon Reservoir when, on 21 April, the Chinese responded with their own spring offensive. A ROK division on their right was swept away, and the Marines were forced to take over their sector. Five days of hard fighting were needed to stabilise the situation.

The Chinese launched a second offensive in mid-May. In spite of some bad moments, this also was a failure. A UN counterstroke brought the 1st Marine Division to a ridgeline overlooking a deep circular valley, immediately nicknamed 'The Punchbowl'. Truce negotiations were now opened, and UN forces settled down in defensive positions.

An uneventful summer ended on 5 September 1951, when the Marines were ordered to capture the rest of the Punchbowl. This was accomplished in 18 days of hard fighting, distinguished only by the first use of helicopters to transport troops in combat. HMR-161, the first Marine transport helicopter squadron, had arrived in Korea with its new HRS-1s just that month. For the first time, Marine commanders lamented the quality of their air support. During the summer, despite vehement protests, the Air Force had taken over operational control of 1st MAW.

The Marines continued to hold the Punchbowl sector throughout the winter of 1951–52. On 23 March 1952 they were moved 180 miles west to the left flank of the UN line, where they would spend the rest of the war. There would be no more general offensives, and day-to-day life came to resemble World War I, with patrols and trench raids on enemy outposts. There were occasional sharp fights as one or another position changed hands: 'Bunker

Hill' in August, 'The Hook' in October. In early 1953 there was a series of battles involving outposts 'Reno', 'Carson', and 'Vegas'. The war ended on 27 July 1953. In three years of fighting the Marines lost 4,262 dead and 21,781 wounded. The 1st Division would remain in Korea until 1955.

The 1950s and 1960s

During the war the Corps had naturally devoted most of its attention to Korea; but the legislative struggle had also continued. In January 1951 the Douglas-Mansfield Bill was introduced into Congress. This established the Marines once and for all as a separate service, and fixed its active establishment at three divisions and three air wings. (A fourth division and another air wing are part of the Reserves.) The Commandant was made a member of the Joint Chiefs of Staff, with co-equal status on matters of concern to the Marine Corps. Truman signed the bill into law on 28 June 1952. The Marines had won 'the right to fight' on the battlefields of Korea.

Gen. Cates retired at the end of 1951, and Lemuel C. Shepherd Jr. was appointed Commandant. The 3rd Division authorised by Congress was activated in January 1952 and deployed to Japan in August 1953. In 1955 the 1st MAW was moved from Korea to Japan, and the 3rd Division had to find new quarters. The 4th Regiment went to Hawaii to become the ground element of the 1st Brigade; the rest of the division went to Okinawa.

Gen. Shepherd retired at the end of 1955, and President Eisenhower named Gen. Randolph M. Pate as his successor. Pate's first crisis came in early April. A Drill Instructor at the Parris Island Recruit Depot took his platoon out for an unauthorised night march, and six of them drowned in Ribbon Creek. The ensuing courtmartial attracted national coverage, and an official inquiry into recruit training methods was ordered. Recommendations set guidelines for Drill Instructors, and some harsh disciplinary practices were eliminated. Oddly enough, Marine recruiting actually went up after the incident.

Abroad, Marines were used to secure the evacuation of American nationals from Alexandria during the Suez crisis of 1956. Units were also put aboard ship during two Venezuelan disorders in

Marine Reconnaissance personnel of the 2nd Div. prepare for a training jump: Camp Lejeune, 1958. M1944 camouflage utilities are worn with brown Army Corcoran Paratroop Boots. Note both plain and camouflage utility caps, and pre-World War II plastic Riddell jump helmet. The M1941 Haversack is strapped below the reserve pack of the T-10 Parachute. Weapons included the M3 'grease gun' SMG and Kabar knives seen here, and the M1 rifle. The left man has a strobe light strapped to his right shin beside the knife. (USMC A340778)

Under the supervision of their Drill Instructor, 1965 recruits at the San Diego Depot practise sighting with M-14 rifles. The special shooting jacket is 'organisational' clothing provided for range weeks. The armband—in company colours of red, blue or yellow—identifies one man as Recruit Guide of Platoon 324. (USMC A229955)

HQ elements of 'India' Co., 3/6 Marines in Santo Domingo, Dominican Republic in May 1965. Radios are (left) AN/PRC-6 and (right) AN/PRC-11. The officer with his back to us displays a rear view of the M1941 Belt Suspenders; the separate straps are connected here with a piece of wire, and a grenade pull-ring was another frequent expedient. He wears two types of canteen: (left) M1956, attaching round the belt, and (right) M1910, hooking to the belt eyelets. (USMC A19576)

early 1958, but in neither case did they land.

On 14 July 1958 the pro-Western King Feisal of Iraq was murdered in a *coup d'état*, and the delicate equilibrium of the whole region was in danger. Half-Christian, half-Moslem Lebanon was facing a possible civil war and Syrian invasion, and its president asked for US intervention. By coincidence, the US 6th Fleet had under its command three Battalion Landing Teams and a provisional brigade headquarters, who had been in the Mediterranean for a landing exercise. BLT 2/2 went ashore on 15 July, placidly observed by bikini-clad bathers and soft-drink vendors, and secured the airfield. BLT 3/6 landed the next day, and the Marines moved into the city to secure communications with the American Embassy. On the 17th, BLT 1/8 landed north of the city and elements of 2/8 were airlifted in from Camp Lejeune. An Army Airborne brigade arrived from Germany,

and its commander assumed control of all US forces present. For once, this went smoothly. The crisis ended, elections were held, and the Marines departed in October.

In the Far East, Communist China was threatening both Taiwan and its offshore islands, and elements of 1st MAW were moved in from Japan. MAG-11's fighters patrolled aggressively; Chinese MiGs were occasionally seen, but invariably fled before they could be engaged. The Communist-inspired civil war in Laos heated up in 1960, and a helicopter squadron was deployed to Thailand in 1962.

At home, joint Navy/Marine tests with the old escort carrier USS *Thetis Bay* helped establish criteria for a new class of amphibious ship, the Helicopter Carrier (LPH). Three World War II *Essex*-class attack carriers—the *Boxer*, *Princeton* and *Valley Forge*—were converted to the new specifications, and specially designed successors were laid down. The first of these, the USS *Iwo Jima*, was commissioned in 1961. FMF forces were also restructured to make landing elements largely helicopter-mobile. A new transport helicopter, the HUS (later H-34) was adopted, and larger designs were also procured in limited numbers. In the late 1950s and early 1960s Marine fixed-wing units also began to receive new equipment: the F-8 Crusader, F-4 Phantom II and A-4 attack 'plane. The C-130 Hercules also entered use, providing not only a much improved transport capacity, but (in its KC-130 version) air-refuelling ability as well.

David Shoup succeeded Pate as Commandant in January 1960. A Medal of Honor winner from Tarawa, Shoup served until 1964. A private opponent of American policy toward Cuba, he also antagonised President Kennedy's 'best and brightest' by opposing US involvement in Vietnam.

In October 1962 President Kennedy presented an ultimatum to the Soviets on removing offensive missiles from Cuba. Marine units were among the forces deployed in support of his action. The garrison at Guantanamo was reinforced to regimental strength, and the rest of the 2nd Division went south to the Caribbean in amphibious ships. From the West Coast came the 5th Marine Expeditionary Brigade, out of the 1st Division via the Panama Canal. The 2nd MAW deployed south to Florida and Puerto Rico, and its reconnaissance pilots began to fly photo missions over Cuba. The crisis was settled without the need for further operations, and the forces returned home.

The Marines were tested again in the Caribbean in April 1965. A coup, allegedly Communist-inspired, was taking place in Santo Domingo, capital of the Dominican Republic. The 6th Marine Expeditionary Unit, with BLT 3/6 and HMM-264 (Helicopter Squadron, Marine, Medium) aboard the LPH *Boxer*, were ordered to evacuate US nationals. The situation was going badly for the loyalists, and they asked for a battalion of Marines to restore order: they could no longer guarantee the security of either the US Embassy or the evacuation site. BLT 3/6 was lifted ashore on 29 April, and Army Airborne troops flew in the next day. Together they established an International Safety Zone within the city. BLT's 1/6 and 1/8 Marines came in by air, while 1/2 remained offshore aboard the LPH *Okinawa*. An Inter-American Peace Force replaced the Americans in May; a new Dominican government was formed; and the Marines were gone in June.

In the early 1960s Marine Air received an extra mission. As Navy attack squadrons converted to more advanced aircraft, a temporary shortage of such units available for carrier deployment occurred. The Marines, normally shore-based, were asked to fill in; and VMA attack units were provided for several years, eventually including the early period of Vietnam operations. At the same time, the expansion of the helicopter arm created a severe pilot shortage for these units. The Marines considered several alternatives, including starting a Warrant Officer Flight Program like the Army's, or resurrecting the pre-World War II concept of enlisted pilots. In the end they decided simply to re-assign fixed-wing pilots to the helicopter units.

Vietnam: the Early Years

Wallace M. Greene Jr. succeeded Shoup as Commandant on 1 January 1964, just as America was becoming seriously involved in Vietnam. Since 1954 the Marines had been providing a tiny Advisory Group to the South Vietnamese Marine Corps. In April 1962 HMM-362 was brought in with 24 UH-34Ds to support the Vietnamese armed forces. Operating from Soc Trang, south-west of Saigon, they flew 4,400 sorties by August, when they were relieved by HMM-163. The project was designated Operation 'Shu-Fly' and moved to Danang in September. The Marines continued to rotate individual squadrons in for six month tours until March 1965, when the war had expanded considerably.

The Landings
The involvement of ground troops began gradually. In August 1964 the Gulf of Tonkin incident, in which North Vietnamese patrol boats attacked US warships at sea, caused the activation of the 9th Marine Expeditionary Brigade in Okinawa, out of assets of the 3rd Marine Division. The war was going badly for the Republic of Vietnam (RVN), and the initial American response was a series of air strikes on North Vietnam (Operation 'Flaming Dart') in February 1965. To forestall any retaliation, the Marine 1st Light Anti-Aircraft Missile Battalion was landed at Danang with its Hawk batteries. The decision to commit ground

Marines of 1/3 arrive by USAF C-130 to begin the US build-up at Danang, RVN, on 8 March 1965. As this was an 'administrative' move, the men wear the complete Field Transport Pack, with bedrolls made up using OD Shelter Halves. Note 3rd MARDIV insignia—the three-point 'caltrop'—painted on the middle man's seabag. (USMC A184402)

troops, initially for defensive purposes only, was made by President Johnson near the end of February. On 8 March 1965 Navy TF 76 received the order: 'Close Danang, land the landing force.' BLT 3/9 waded ashore through moderate surf at 9am, and moved out to a ridgeline west of the airfield. With them came Brig. Gen. Frederick J. Karch, 9th MEB commander, and his staff. The same afternoon BLT 1/3 came in from Okinawa by Air Force C-130. The next day the LPH Princeton, standing off the coast, flew off 23 UH-34s of HMM-365 in support.

Additional reinforcements arrived in April: BLT 2/3 and VMFA-531 (a Phantom unit) for Danang on 11 April, and BLT 3/4 for Phu Bai three days later. The decision to use the Marine Corps in Vietnam's northern provinces was made on the recommendation of Gen. William Westmoreland, senior US commander in Vietnam. His chief reason involved logistics; in 1965 Vietnam had only one

deep-water port in operation—Saigon—and that would be needed to support other Free World military forces. The Marines, however, could support themselves over the beach. Secondly, the Marines were weak in support units and might have trouble sustaining operations over long distances. I Corps (the Vietnamese military designation for their five northernmost provinces), with its relatively limited area, offered the best opportunity to minimise this problem. Westmoreland also hoped for a chance to employ the famous Marine amphibious capability; and felt that their rifle companies, larger than Army companies, would be useful in case of direct North Vietnamese intervention.

On 3 May the 3rd Marine Division moved its headquarters to Danang. Three days later, 9th MEB was dissolved to become III Marine Amphibious Force—'III MAF' to a generation of Marines. On 7 May the rest of the 3rd Division—the Hawaii-based 3rd MEB (4th Marines and MAG-12)—arrived by sea. Originally put aboard ship for a landing exercise in California, the unit was instead diverted to Okinawa while at sea. The 3rd MEB landed at Chu Lai, on a pine-fringed beach 55 miles south of Danang; and under its protection, Marine engineers and Navy Seabees began construction of an airfield. On 11 May the headquarters of 1st MAW also arrived at Danang. Maj. Gen. Lewis W. Walt assumed command of Marine forces in Vietnam on 4 June.

With the 3rd Division now committed to Vietnam, the 1st was staged forward from Camp Pendleton to take their place. The 5th Marines went to Hawaii and the 7th to Okinawa. On 1 July, while acting as the 7th Fleet's Special Landing Force, BLT 3/7 went ashore at Qui Nhon to establish a fourth Marine enclave.

Throughout the summer of 1965 new units arrived. By August the 3rd, 4th, 7th and 9th Marine Regiments were in-country, supported by four Marine Air Groups. Two airfields were in

Marines of Co.C, 1/5, with a captured Viet Cong sniper at Trung Tin, Vietnam, in December 1966. They wear a mixture of ordinary and jungle utilities, M1955 Armor Vests, and M1961 webbing gear; note M1942 field dressing pouches. (USMC A369730)

operation: Danang, and a new SATS field at Chu Lai (using carrier technology to operate jet aircraft from a short runway). In September a new helicopter facility opened at Marble Mountain near Danang.

The Marines carried out their first major operation in August, when an intelligence windfall pinpointed the 1st Viet Cong Regiment's location south of Chu Lai. A pincer operation was quickly improvised under control of the 7th Regiment, involving amtracks, helicopters and amphibious shipping of Navy TF 76. In the course of the operation, designated 'Starlite', the 7th controlled not only its own 1/7, but also 2/4 and 3/3 and the 7th Fleet's SLF, BLT 3/7. Over 1,000 Viet Cong were killed, and it was forcibly demonstrated to the

enemy that even his Main Force units could not stand up to the Marines in a pitched battle. The Command and Control arrangements also set a pattern for the rest of the war, with Regimental headquarters functioning in the same fashion as Army Brigades, controlling a varying complement of subordinate units.

For the rest of the year, however, the Marines conducted few large operations, preferring to concentrate on local security sweeps in the immediate vicinity of their bases. This strategy brought them into conflict with Headquarters, USARV (United States Army, Vietnam) and Gen. Westmoreland. In its own areas the Army had immediately embarked on a series of clearing operations (unfortunately designated 'Search and Destroy' missions) in traditional VC base areas. They wished the Marines to do the same; but Walt demurred. On arrival in Vietnam, the Marines had been appalled at the number of civilians to be found

Marines of the 7th Fleet's SLF (Special Landing Force) cross a river during Operation 'Deckhouse VI' in February 1967. Note AN/PRC-11 radio on its special packframe; the battery box has been decorated with the 3rd MARDIV insignia. (USMC A191159)

A Marine machine gunner advances through waist-deep foliage while on patrol in Vietnam. Note folded nylon rain poncho stowed beneath his pack straps, a common field practice. (USMC)

For early Vietnam operations, Marine helicopter crews generally wore these uniforms: ordinary utilities for door gunners, and crew chiefs, and khaki Summer Flying Coveralls for pilots. (USMC A422192)

in the immediate vicinity of their bases. With his units spread so thin, Walt felt that he could not embark on such operations without first securing his base areas.

A dramatic VC attack on Marble Mountain and Chu Lai on the night of 27 October seemed to vindicate this view. A platoon of sappers infiltrated the airfield under cover of a mortar attack. About 46 were killed by the defenders, but six survived to reach the flightline: 19 helicopters were destroyed and 11 damaged, including all but four of the new UH-1E gunships which the Marines had in-country. The VC were less successful at Chu Lai, where the Marines lost two A-4s. Unfortunately, experience would establish that no American defence was totally successful in preventing this sort of attack.

During the autumn monsoon the Marines were twice called on to rescue major ARVN (Army of the Republic of Vietnam) units under enemy attack. Some limited operations of their own were also conducted, but much of III MAF's energy was still devoted to pacification. Starting with 3/4 at Phu

Bai, Combined Action Companies were established in areas cleared by Marine combat operations. This programme assigned 14-man Marine rifle squads to work within Vietnamese Popular Force platoons to provide hamlet security. More troops were clearly needed, however, and in January 1966 the decision was made to deploy the rest of the 1st Marine Division to Vietnam. Its 7th Regiment and two battalions of the 1st were already in-country and the rest had arrived, battalion by battalion, by June. In March, 1st MARDIV officially set up headquarters at Chu Lai.

1966—North to the DMZ

In early April 1966 the Marines were faced with yet another crisis, this time of a political nature. On 10 March the Saigon military council removed the I Corps commander, Maj. Gen. Thi. Anti-government riots erupted in Danang and Hue under Buddhist leadership. Premier Ky responded by bringing three battalions of Vietnamese Marines to Danang. Rebellious ARVN units threatened to attack the airbase, but a battalion of American

The CS/FRP-1 fire-resistant coveralls were introduced in 1967; these H-34 crewmen wear them in 1968, by which time the Mk.II Life Preserver was rarely seen in Vietnam. The new coveralls replaced earlier types for both fixed-wing and helicopter crews of the Marine Corps. (USMC A422212)

Marines dissuaded them. An accommodation of sorts was reached which lasted until mid-May, when reinforced Ky forces overran the dissidents' headquarters in the city. After a week of heavy fighting the crisis ended in a government victory, but the revolt had played havoc with pacification throughout I Corps.

In the first three months of 1966 the Marines continued large operations only in support of contacts developed by the ARVN (Operations 'New York', 'Utah', 'Texas' and 'Indiana'). Starting in March, under their new commander Maj. Gen. W. B. Kyle, the 3rd Division began multi-battalion clearing operations south of Danang to An Hoa.

In July, following up intelligence reports of PAVN (People's Army of Vietnam—the North Vietnamese Army proper) units near the DMZ, the Marines began Operation 'Hastings', which lasted until August. Under control of TF DELTA, six

Marine battalions (including the SLF) defeated five battalions of the PAVN 324th Division's tough, Chinese-equipped troops. Two weeks later the 324th tried again, this time with the 341st to assist. Operation 'Prairie' continued against this second effort in four phases until June 1967, in the strip between Route 9 and the DMZ.

Marine reinforcements that year included the Korean 9th 'Blue Dragon' Marine Brigade; but the Marines were running short of units. A decision had been made not to activate the Reserves, so instead the 5th Marine Division was re-activated at Camp Pendleton, California. By the end of the year its first regiment, the 26th Marines, was staging forward to the Western Pacific. The 1st MARDIV moved north to Phu Bai in October the better to control the border battles, and the 3rd moved up to Danang. Chu Lai was left to the ROK 'Blue Dragons' and two battalions of Marine TF X-RAY. In April 1967 Army units of TF OREGON relieved the Marines in southern I Corps.

1st MAW's air assets had also been increased. In 1966 new CH-46 medium helicopters arrived to supplant the UH-34s. Even larger CH-53s arrived in early 1967. The first Marine squadron of all-weather A-6A attack 'planes also began flying from Danang in late 1966. Once the Marines began fixed-wing operations in Vietnam, an old question arose. The Air Force insisted they had the right to control Marine air operations; the Marines, leery of their Korean experience, resisted. A compromise was achieved, and 1st MAW was allowed to decide which air assets would be available for joint missions. A conflict also arose over the A-6s. Most Marine missions were flown in-country, but the Navy wanted the A-6s used exclusively for night operations against the Ho Chi Minh Trail. Again, a compromise was reached.

Operations in 1967

On the ground, 1967 began with minor operations along Highway 1. 'Prairie' continued in the north, the longest and bloodiest Marine operation of the war. 'Deckhouse V', latest in a series of 7th Fleet SLF operations on the coast, opened in a new area—the Mekong Delta south of Saigon. At the same time, III MAF established a rotation policy, exchanging units with the 9th Marine Amphibious Brigade in Okinawa on a periodic basis. (The word

The battle for Hue: Marine gunners manhandle their 106mm recoilless rifle through a demolished garden for a better shot at the dug-in enemy, February 1968. (USMC)

Marines of 2/26 wade a stream near Hoi An during Operation 'Valiant Hunt' in December 1968. The configuration of the pack is unusual: the Knapsack was rarely used in Vietnam. The small bag is a shaving kit. Note field dressings in helmet band. (USMC A192504)

'Expeditionary' had been dropped from Marine designations the year before.) In late February, new types of Soviet 140mm rockets struck Danang Main. April and May saw heavy fighting in the Que Son Valley during Operation 'Union'. By 1967 the war had become a confusing series of codenames and statistics. One name that first appeared in April was Khe Sanh.

On 24 April a patrol from 1/9 encountered an NVA force near the outpost and its small airstrip, apparently preparing for an attack. The next day 3/3 came in by helicopter, and was heavily engaged before nightfall. The 3rd Marines' command group and 2/3 arrived the next day as reinforcements. Supported by air strikes and artillery, they pushed the NVA off the hills in two weeks of bitter fighting.

The 325B Division lost a reported 940 dead. With the battle ended, the newly arrived 26th Marines were brought in as replacements for the 3rd. The Marines then went over to the offensive along the DMZ in Operations 'Hickory' and 'Prairie IV'.

In late May and June 9th MAB, 1st MARDIV and 1st MAW all received new commanders. The biggest change, however, came when Lt. Gen. Robert E. Cushman, Jr. relieved Gen. Walt as Marine commander in Vietnam. Changes also occurred for the ground troops. The controversial M-16 rifle replaced the M-14 just prior to the Khe Sanh 'hill fights', but initial problems with reliability made many Marines regret the change.

Attention turned from Khe Sanh in July. In late 1966, Secretary of Defense Robert MacNamara announced that the US would create an electronic and sensor barrier along the DMZ to deter infiltration; this was dubbed 'The MacNamara Line' by the Press. Work began in the spring. The western terminus was Con Thien, held by one battalion of Marines less than five miles from the DMZ. In July the NVA began operations against it, supported by artillery from across the border. Con Thien received much shelling and an occasional ground probe, but massive air strikes and aggressive Marine ground operations defeated enemy at-

A .50cal. machine gunner of the Force Logistical Command test-fires his weapon before the start of a 1969 supply convoy from Danang. He wears a hooded US Navy rain jacket over camouflage utilities, and an M69 Armor Vest is draped over the seat. (USMC)

tempts to approach the perimeter. The NVA gave up in late September.

Marine Air faced its own crisis in the fall of 1967. After a series of tragic accidents, the CH-46 helicopter was grounded for extensive modifications. Since they comprised nearly half the cargo and personnel lift capacity of the Marines in-country, their loss was keenly felt. The modified aircraft were returned to service in December. New M-16 rifles, also modified, were issued by the end of October.

3rd MARDIV personnel photographed during Operation 'Golden Fleece', October 1965. Note 40mm grenade bandoliers visible below slung M-79 launcher on right. (USMC A186014)

The year ended with 1st MARDIV operations south of Danang. Maj. Gen. Hochmuth, 3rd MARDIV commander, was killed in a helicopter crash on 14 November, two weeks after receiving the Presidential Unit Citation for his division in Danang from Vice-President Humphrey. Twenty-one battalions of three Marine divisions were now in-country.

1968: Khe Sanh and Tet

By the beginning of 1968, Khe Sanh had become a backwater of the war. A beerhall had even been built. On 20 January a patrol from 3/26 encountered a North Vietnamese battalion at the scene of the previous year's hill fighting. Rumours had persisted of an imminent NVA attack on one of the Marine Combat Bases near the DMZ. Gen. Cushman decided to reinforce the base, but only to the extent that it could be supplied by air. Even this was a risk, since the same monsoon rains that closed Route 9 could also impede air operations. By mid-January all three battalions of the 26th Marines (Col. David Lownds) were in place. At Lownds's request another battalion was added; 1/9, veteran of the spring 'Hill Fights'. A very weak ARVN 37th Ranger Battalion came in late in January. On 21 January the NVA took Khe Sanh village, and the siege was on.

Khe Sanh's predicament attracted worldwide Press attention. In Washington, President Lyndon Johnson requested a letter in writing from the Joint Chiefs of Staff guaranteeing that the base could be held. At the end of the month the NVA announced another of their usual holiday truces, this one for the Vietnamese lunar New Year, the *Têt*.

On the night of 30 January the VC and NVA suddenly struck. Their co-ordinated attacks were aimed not at military bases, but at cities. In spite of surprise and previously infiltrated units, the attacks against the provincial capitals of Tam Ky, Quang Ngai and Quang Tri cities failed. At Danang, a full-scale attack by the NVA 2nd Division was detected by reconnaissance elements of 1st MARDIV. Air and artillery were brought to bear as the NVA debouched from foothills west of An Hoa, and they were driven back with heavy losses. Within the city, a VC attack on ARVN Headquarters was beaten

Marines on patrol south-west of Danang in May 1970. T-shirts and minimal equipment were the norm for short-range operations at this time. (USMC A373687)

off by Vietnamese Rangers and Marine support troops. Only in Hue was the enemy successful.

The former Imperial capital, the coastal city of Hue was divided north and south by the Perfume River. The north side was dominated by the Citadel, three miles square and surrounded by thick walls and a medieval-looking moat. Just south of the river were a cluster of government buildings, Hue University and the MACV (Military Assistance Command, Vietnam) advisors' compound. On the night of 30/31 January the infiltrators took it all, except the MACV compound, and the ARVN 1st Division Headquarters in the north-west corner of the Citadel.

First reports trickled into Phu Bai, ten miles south of Hue, just as the base was hit by an NVA rocket attack. With the situation unclear, only a small relief force was initially despatched, built around

25

Draped with extra bandoliers and LAAW rockets, Marines of 3/26 search the ground north-west of Danang in January 1970. The long pouch slung behind the shoulder of the left hand man holds the bipod and cleaning kit for the M-16. (USMC A374157)

Company A, 1/1 Marines. It was ambushed on the outskirts of the city. Reinforcements arrived, and the MACV compound was relieved at noon. An attempt to reach the ARVN headquarters across the river was stopped at the bridge. By then the seriousness of the situation was appreciated, and further units were despatched. It took until 10 February for elements of 1/1 and 2/5 Marines to clear the government buildings south of the river, literally house by house. The task was all the harder because of a decision not to use air strikes, artillery or naval gunfire in the city.

Across the river, the ARVN were making little progress against the Citadel. On 12 February they requested Marine assistance, and 1/5 went in on the left flank. After ten days of gruelling combat the walls were at last breached. The ARVN were given the honour of the final assault; and the battle of Hue was declared over in early March. Between eight and 11 NVA battalions had been destroyed; but much of the beautiful city lay in ruins.

The enemy's Tet Offensive had been a public relations success, but a military disaster. Everywhere he attacked, he had been defeated with heavy losses.

Attention now shifted to Khe Sanh, where the NVA persisted in their siege, employing the classic tactics of trenches, zig-zags and parallels. Under fire from artillery emplaced across the Laos border, the Marines ceased patrolling outside their perimeter. Not all the base defences were inside the wire, however. The Marines' main weapon was actually a co-ordinated fireplan, codenamed 'Niagara'. It employed artillery of various calibres, tactical air and even B-52 strikes to break up enemy concentrations and defend the base. The opportunity to test this came on 5 February. Sensors detected a major enemy movement toward the perimeter during the early morning hours. The fireplan was employed with devastating effect. Only one enemy battalion was able to attack, and ground defences stopped it on the wire. The next night, however, an NVA infantry regiment, led by tanks and flamethrowers, assaulted the Army's nearby

Lang Vei Special Forces Camp and killed or routed its defenders.

1968: Later Operations

The next morning Gen. Westmoreland himself flew to Danang to meet with Marine and Army commanders in I Corps. The 7 February agenda began with discussion of a relief force for Lang Vei, but Westmoreland had other things on his mind. Since mid-1967 Army units had also been operating in I Corps, with TF OREGON upgraded to divisional size in September (as the Americal Division). Later in the year, concerned about the situation at the DMZ, Westmoreland ordered further Army units into I Corps. These included elements of the 101st Airborne Division and the 1st Cavalry Division (Airmobile). In February, of the 52 US infantry battalions in I Corps (over half of all such units in-country), 24 were Marine but 28 were Army.

Westmoreland had originally placed these units at the disposal of III MAF, but the Marines had largely ignored them. The Army were issued no orders; no joint operations were proposed; no liaison officers had been provided; and Marine units even kept Army ones out of their radio nets. As the Army was now providing not only most of the infantry, but much of the support in I Corps, the situation was intolerable. Westmoreland had two solutions for this. Firstly, he simply ordered Cushman's subordinates to co-operate with Army units. Secondly he established a branch of his own headquarters (USARV Forward, shortly, XXIV Corps) to control Army units in I Corps. This HQ he placed under III MAF in March 1968.

The other issue the conference raised was an old question: control of Marine Air. Since their previous understanding with the Air Force the Marines had, on two occasions, agreed to place their fixed-wing assets temporarily under joint control. One of these exceptions was 'Niagara'. The other was 'Slam', a similar plan used at Con Thien. Regarding the practice of setting up and dissolving special command arrangements as wasteful, Westmoreland now wanted control of all Marine aircraft, except helicopters, permanently passed to 7th Air Force. This question went all the way back to Washington and the new Commandant, Leonard F. Chapman, Jr. The question was

discussed by the Joint Chiefs of Staff and never formally resolved, but in March the Marines began working under 7th Air Force control.

The first joint operation was 'Pegasus', the relief of Khe Sanh. On 1 April, while the 1st Marines and three ARVN battalions advanced along Route 9, helicopters of the Army's 1st Cavalry Division leap-frogged forward, establishing a series of firebases to support their advance. With the monsoon ending, the NVA had made a final, futile ground attack on the night of 30 March, and then melted away before the advance. The base was relieved on 6 April, and 45 days of artillery bombardment ended on the 9th. Total Marine casualties had been 205 dead, 1,668 wounded. Four aircraft and 17 helicopters had been shot down. Enemy casualties were unknown, but the two ground attacks had piled up 1,602 enemy dead along the wire. It was thought that perhaps 10–15,000 had perished under air strikes and artillery.

Beneath the wing of their A-6 attack aircraft, Marine pilots of VMA(AW)-242 accept a ceremonial glass of champagne at Danang after completing their unit's 15,000th mission in March 1970. They wear Z-4 Anti-G Suits with leg restraints, MA-2 cutaway Torso Harness, Mk.2 Life Preservers and early SV-2 Survival Vests. (USMC A422552)

Marines of 2/9 case their Regimental Colors as they prepare to depart from Vietnam in August 1969. They wear camouflage utilities, Army M1956 webbing gear, Marine Jungle First Aid Pouches and M1961 Ammunition Pouches. Note that one man still wears the World War II/Korean War vintage camouflage helmet cover. (USMC 3M-5-1355-69)

Army units pressed into the A Shau valley in April and May. Meanwhile, 3rd MARDIV fought a six-day battle near Dong Ha against the 320th NVA Division; and in June, TF HOTEL (1st and 4th Marines) carried out operations against the 320th south of Khe Sanh. The Combat Base itself was abandoned in early July, a controversial decision made possible only by the arrival of the more mobile Army units in I Corps. The base itself was no longer needed to support operations in the Western DMZ.

As post-Tet reinforcements, Cushman had received the 27th Marines and one battalion of the 13th in late February. Three battalions came in by air from Pendleton, and 1/27, out of 1st MAB in Hawaii, was diverted while at sea on a landing exercise. Only two battalions and 5th MARDIV headquarters at Pendleton now remained in FMF-Pacific Reserve. The 27th, assigned a coastal sector, took part in Operation 'Allen Brook' in May.

After the violence of the early months, summer 1968 passed quietly while the NVA withdrew to lick their wounds. The Army's 5th Mechanized Division arrived in August, allowing the 27th Marines to depart in September. The 1st Cavalry Division deployed south before the monsoon, and remaining units adjusted their boundaries accordingly. Gen. Westmoreland left in July to become Army Chief of Staff; Gen. Creighton Abrams took his place. In the second half of 1968 the Marines again turned their attention to pacification.

Withdrawal

President Richard Nixon took office on 20 January 1969, and the emphasis of US efforts in Vietnam shifted towards support of the ARVN and preparations for withdrawal. The Marines' last big operations took place in the first three months of the year. In January, 'Bold Mariner' was conducted south of Chu Lai, using the SLF and part of the Americal Division. In March, by concentrating his helicopter assets, Cushman was able to carry out an Army-style airmobile operation—'Dewey Canyon I'—in Quang Tri province, using three battalions of the 9th Marines. Cushman left in March, and Lt.

The small Marine advisory group with the Vietnamese Marine Corps were among the last US personnel to serve in Vietnam: in 1954, they had been among the first. This USMC major is seen with a VNMC doctor in Quang Tri City in 1972. The officers wear two different versions of 'tiger-stripe' uniform; note pocket differences, and the American officer's extra trousers pockets outside the knees. In addition to the non-standard 'U.S.MARINES' nametape the advisor wears a personal nametape in his VNMC battalion colour; the VNMC patch on his left shoulder—obscured here, but see Vietnamese officer; and a brigade patch, and VNMC rank insignia, on his right pocket. Note black US Army web belt. (USN 1154735)

Gen. Herman Nickerson took his place.

The first major US troop withdrawals involved the 9th Marines, who returned to Okinawa in July 1969. Before they departed an exchange of personnel with other units was carried out, so that only personnel normally scheduled for rotation actually left. The rest of 3rd MARDIV was gone by mid-October, and the 26th Marines by April 1970. Lt. Gen. Keith McCutcheon, a helicopter pioneer, replaced Nickerson in March. On his arrival, III MAF and XXIV Corps changed places, with the former now subordinate to the latter.

Only the three regiments of the 1st MARDIV remained. In September 1970 they took part in their last operation, 'Imperial Lake', in support of the ARVN. Gen. McCutcheon returned to the US

on medical leave in November (he died of cancer six months later), and Lt. Gen. Donn Robertson arrived to become the last III MAF commander. The 5th and 7th Marines departed, and III MAF was replaced in April by 3rd MAB, comprising only the 1st Marines and supporting elements. The last Marine unit was gone by July 1971, leaving only embassy guards, advisors, and some technical personnel still in-country: about 500 in all.

The 1972 Communist Easter Offensive brought back Marine aviation units, MAG-12 and -15, but no ground troops were employed. Other Marine squadrons operated from Navy carriers in the Gulf of Tonkin. Eight years of war in Vietnam had cost the Marines 12,936 dead and 88,594 wounded.

After withdrawal, the 1st Division returned to California and the 3rd to Okinawa and Hawaii (1st MAB). The 5th was again decommissioned, and the 2nd remained on the East Coast, supported by the 2nd Marine Air Wing. The 1st MAW was redeployed to Japan and Okinawa, and the 3rd remained at El Toro, California.

The 1970s: Rebuilding the Corps

Gen. Cushman took over as Marine Commandant on 1 January 1972. He inherited a Corps in serious difficulty. In a country profoundly traumatised by Vietnam, even the Corps' traditional missions seemed discredited. There was much Press criticism of Vietnam casualties and racial discord. There was the problem of modernisation in an era of shrinking budgets and rising costs, and of maintaining authorised strength without the stimulus of conscription. If Cushman could not expect to solve all these problems, he at least had to make a start.

His first concern was to re-establish the Corps' amphibious mission: 'We're pulling our heads out of the jungle and getting back into the amphibious business. . .'. This was going to be a problem. The Navy had its own budget reductions to worry about, and had no plans to replace most of its World War II vintage amphibious shipping as it was scrapped. A new class of ship was introduced, the *Tarawa*-class LHA, which could carry landing craft as well as helicopters; and some other new types also

Since the late 1970s the camouflage utility uniform, worn by these aircraft mechanics, has been standard working dress on all Marine installations. (USMC)

entered service. The Marines also worried about the decline of the naval gun in favour of guided missiles; and even more about potential shortages of aircraft carriers and escort ships. In the future, amphibious task forces might have to defend themselves against a variety of threats, and guns, missiles, close-in defence systems and VSTOL aircraft were added to the ships' designs. By the 1980s, amphibious vessels were rapidly acquiring a 'one-man band' look.

Press criticism of Vietnam operations convinced the Marines that they might no longer be able to employ massive firepower, nor accept heavy losses on future battlefields, with equanimity. (While public reaction against the scale of American combat casualties was general, it was particularly relevant to the Marine Corps, whose traditional philosophy of accepting high casualties as the cost of fulfilling their missions was noted by many observers in Vietnam.) The Corps began looking

into new electronics, command and control systems, radios, computers and laser systems in an effort to 'fight smarter'. As a by-product of this programme, an effort was made to enlist Marines who scored high on qualifying tests, rather than those who had completed High School.

Personnel problems occupied much attention in the early 1970s. The Corps had not adequately prepared for the end of conscription, and fell seriously below recruiting goals in 1974. In an effort to catch up, a number of undesirables were permitted to enlist, creating disciplinary problems once they were assigned to units. Retention of NCOs was a continuing concern.

Traditional missions continued for the Corps in the 1970s. FMF-Atlantic units stood by for possible use during the 1973 Yom Kippur War, and helped evacuate foreign nationals during the Cyprus crisis the following year. In April 1975, Marines returned to South-East Asia to assist in the final evacuations from Cambodia and Saigon (Operations 'Eagle Pull' and 'Frequent Wind', respectively) as those countries fell to the Communists. In May they

One unexpected result of the 1970s joint training exercises in Northern Europe has been the adoption of the British 'woolly pully' sweater. After admiring the sweaters worn by the Royal Marine Commandos, their American counterparts adopted the garment to replace an unpopular windcheater-style jacket then in use. This Military Policeman wears it with enlisted Winter 'B' uniform, MP badge, and a red and yellow brassard. (USMC)

Personnel of the 2nd Marine Regiment at Camp Lejeune in 1978 wear slanted-pocket camouflage utilities with 'woodland' pattern helmet covers, and LC-1 personal equipment but with M1956 Belt Suspenders. (USMC A454261)

helped recover the captured US merchant vessel *Mayaguez* and her crew from Communist hands.

Gen. Cushman chose to retire early as Commandant; and on the day Saigon fell, 30 April 1975, President Ford nominated Lt. Gen. Louis Wilson as his successor. Wilson, a surprise choice, formally took office on 1 July, a few months short of the Marines' 200th Birthday.

Wilson made a number of changes in Cushman's policies. He cancelled many of the high technology systems Cushman had ordered (including 68 F-14 fighters which the Navy had persuaded him to take), and reversed the policy on non-High School graduates, greatly improving discipline. He tried to buy more British-designed Harrier VSTOL fighters, but the Department of Defense turned him down. He obtained new tanks, artillery and anti-tank weapons for the FMF, but at a cost of deferring other projects to the 1990s. In the late 1970s it was assumed that there would be little need for a purely intervention force, and the Corps' preoccupations began to take on a decidedly European slant. The Marines increased their participation in NATO exercises, training for their wartime mission of operations on Europe's northern flank.

At home, Wilson reacted to several training scandals by tightening controls on Drill Instructors and decreasing harassment of recruits, a controversial change made possible only by higher recruiting standards. There was a new emphasis on large-scale exercises for the FMF, often conducted at the Marines' huge training base at Twenty-Nine Palms, California.

The 1980s

Wilson was succeeded by Lt. Gen. Robert H. Barrow in July 1979. The new Commandant continued Wilson's policies, aided by a new national concern with foreign policy. During the Iran crisis President Carter established the new Rapid Deployment Force, with the Marines as the primary ground element and a Marine general, Paul X. Kelley, as the first commander. The Army soon got its paratroops included, and its own candidate replaced Kelley, but the point had been made. A 12,000-man Ready Brigade remains part of the RDF, its supplies pre-positioned aboard cargo ships at Diego Garcia in the Indian Ocean.

Marines on duty in Beirut display to advantage the PASGT armour vest, the 'woodland' camouflage clothing and accessories, and the LC-1 personal equipment. (USMC)

Gen. Kelley became 28th Commandant in July 1983. Aside from its RDF commitments, the Marine Corps remains the country's most economical defence investment, providing 15 per cent of America's combat divisions and 12 per cent of its tactical aircraft for less than four per cent of the defence budget.

Lebanon and Grenada

In the summer of 1982 the Marines became involved again in Lebanon. The Israeli spring invasion had trapped large PLO (Palestine Liberation Organisation) forces in Beirut, and US forces were among those requested to secure their evacuation. Marines from 32nd MAU's (Marine Amphibious Unit) BLT 2/8 went ashore on 24 August. The mission was completed and the troops withdrawn by early September. A few weeks later, however, they were ordered back as part of a Multi-national Peacekeeping Force, after the Sabra/Shatilla massacres. In October they were relieved by 24th MAU, and the two units would alternate duty at 'The Root' over the next year. (In the meantime, 32nd MAU was re-designated 22nd MAU). Incidents occurred with both Israeli forces and Lebanese militias, but would worsen considerably after 24th MAU's return to Lebanon in May 1983. A terrorist bomb destroyed the US Embassy, and soon the Marine compound was under occasional mortar, rocket and artillery fire. Patrols were harassed by snipers, and casualties taken. Then, on the morning of 23 October, an unknown terrorist drove a truck filled with explosive into the headquarters of BLT 1/8 and blew it, and himself, to pieces. No less than 245 Marines and Navy personnel were killed as they slept, and 130 others wounded. A similar attack against the French contingent killed 58 French paratroopers and injured many more. Even as rescue operations took place, replacement personnel were flown in from Camp Lejeune.

Two days later, Marines from 22nd MAU were in action on Grenada, when the Caribbean island's

1

2

3

A

1:    1st Lt., White Dress 'A', 1983
2:    Staff Sgt., Blue-White Dress 'A', 1975
3:    Musician, US Marine Band, 1983

B

C

1:    Lt. Col., Summer Service 'A', 1956
2:    Cpl., Summer Service 'B', 1961
3:    Drill Instructor, Summer Service 'C', 1983

1

2

3

D

1: 1st Lt., Winter Service 'A', 1952
2: Sgt., Summer Service Dress, 1960
3: Sgt., Blue Dress 'B', 1966

E

Korea, summer 1950:
1:   Tank commander
2:   Machine gunner
3:   Rifleman

F

Korea:
1: Rifleman, winter dress
2: Officer, spring 1951
3: BAR gunner, 1953

G

1:    Force Recon, 1955
2:    Sgt., Lebanon, 1958
3:    Officer, 1958

H

Vietnam, 1965-66:
1:    Sgt., 1st Recon Bn.
2:    Rifleman
3:    Grenadier

Vietnam, 1967-70:
1: Machine gunner
2: Rifleman
3: Helicopter crewman

J

1: Grenadier, Lebanon, 1983
2: Recon Marine, Camp Lejeune, 1983
3: Armoured crewman, 1983

K

Marine pilots:
1: Corsair, VMF-214; Korea, 1950
2: Crusader, VMF(AW)-235; Vietnam, 1966
3: Harrier, VMA-231, 1976

L

Communist government was overthrown in a bizarre coup and US citizens were felt to be in danger. BLT 2/8 landed by helicopter from the LPH *Guam*, quickly seizing all their objectives and assisting Army Rangers in evacuating nearly 1,000 US nationals. The 22nd MAU then re-embarked and continued on to the Mediterranean for the scheduled relief of its sister 24th MAU.

A few days later, President Ronald Reagan spoke at a memorial ceremony for the dead of Lebanon and Grenada:

'America seeks no new territory, nor do we wish to dominate others. Yet we commit our resources and risk the lives of those in our armed forces to rescue others from bloodshed and turmoil, and to prevent humankind from drowning in a sea of tyranny.

'Today, the world looks to America for leadership. And America looks to its Corps of Marines. . .'.

Further Reading

Because of the great interest in the US Marine Corps and its history, many excellent works are devoted to the subject. For the period since World War II, the author particularly recommends the publications of the History and Museums Division, Headquarters, US Marine Corps, Washington DC. Several dozen of these relate to specific campaigns, units and subject areas. Examples include:

The Marines in Vietnam, 1954–1973: An Anthology and Annotated Bibliography.

Marines and Helicopters, 1962–1973.

US Marines in Vietnam: The Advisory and Combat Assistance Era, 1954–1964.

US Marines in Vietnam: The Landing and The Buildup, 1965.

The Battle for Khe Sanh.

Marine Full and Service Dress, 1951. Left to right: Enlisted Dress Blues; Green Winter Service Uniform; Summer Khaki Shirt and Trousers; Enlisted Overcoat; Enlisted Raincoat. (USMC A43214)

These publications, and many others on the Marine Corps, are available from The Superintendent of Documents, US Government Printing Office, Washington DC 20402, USA.

The Plates

Marine Uniforms since 1945

Marine uniforms, aside from combat ('utility') clothing, are designated as either Service Dress or Dress Uniforms. Service Dress is divided into Summer and Winter versions; Dress Uniforms include Evening, Mess, Blue, White and Blue-White uniforms. Each of these categories is further broken down into alphabetically designated sub-variants, with the 'A' Uniforms being the most elaborate within each grouping. There is also the usual distinction between male and female, and officer and enlisted ranks. This results in designations such as Male Enlisted Blue Dress 'C', or Woman Officer's Winter Service Dress 'A'. Simple in theory, in practice the system sometimes confuses even the users. It should also be remembered that the designations are continually changed as new

uniforms are phased in and older ones withdrawn.

In selecting subjects for the colour plates, it was regretfully decided to omit coverage of mess and evening dress, as well as certain other ceremonial uniforms. Many of these are very striking and attractive, and the interested reader is referred to a series of beautiful plates recently completed by Marine Capt. Donna Neary. Intended to accompany the current regulations, they depict literally every type of Dress, Service and Combat uniform currently in use by the Marine Corps. They are available, in colour, from The Superintendent of Documents, US Government Printing Office, Washington DC 20402, USA.

A1: Captain, Blue Dress 'B', 1970
The famous Marine Blue Dress Uniform—the colour has been traditional for most of the Marines' history. Other features recall past successes. The Mameluke sword, for example, commemorates one presented in 1805 by the Pasha of Tripoli to Marine

Members of the Marine Band, Washington DC, May 1950, wearing the Red and White Summer band uniform. There are slight differences from current regulations, e.g. chevrons are no longer worn with this uniform. (USMC 313977)

Lt. O'Bannon for the capture of Derna. The red trouser stripe, worn only by officers and NCOs, traditionally represents the bloody battle of Chapultepec in the Mexican War: it is $1\frac{1}{2}$ins. wide for company and field grade officers, and 2ins. wide for general officers. Majors and above also wear gold braid on hat visors. Since the end of World War II the only major change to this uniform has been a 1963 directive which changed the colour of all Marine leather items (shoes, cap frames, gloves, etc.) from brown to black.

A2: Staff Sergeant, Blue Dress 'B', 1957

One of the first post-war uniform changes was the 1946 re-introduction of the Blue Dress uniform for enlisted men. (Its wear, except for some special cases, had been suspended during World War II.) The new uniform differed from its pre-war predecessor in the addition of pockets to the jacket: formerly, this was a feature of the officer's uniform only. Otherwise the styling differs little from enlisted uniforms worn at the turn of the century. The $1\frac{1}{8}$in. red trouser stripe is worn by NCOs—corporals and above. The blue cloth belt is worn as walking-out dress; the white belt and full-dress buckle are usually prescribed for ceremonies. The hat is actually a frame, worn with different covers. The blue one shown was abolished in 1957, and only the white is now used. The service stripes below the chevrons represent the completion of two previous four-year enlistments. Before 1958, weapons qualification badges were awarded slightly differently from current practice. This NCO's badges indicate that he qualified as Marksman with his M-1 rifle and BAR, and Sharpshooter with the carbine. His ribbons indicate service from the end of World War II through Korea. The swagger stick, carried by officers and staff NCOs (staff sergeant and above), was a pet project of Marine Commandant Pate, and became virtually a required item during his tenure.

A3: Lance Corporal, Blue Dress 'C', 1973

According to regulations, Blue Dress 'C' may be prescribed by local commands authorised to wear the Blue Uniform. Usually 'Blue Charlie' is worn as a duty uniform in summer, and is not authorised for wear off-base. When worn on State Department Posts, the white web Military Police Belt and Buckle

This tan-khaki uniform was worn as Enlisted Summer Service Dress between 1946 and 1952, and by officers between 1946 and 1954. (USMC 308139)

Parris Island recruit platoon in the midst of a pre-graduation drill competition. The Drill Instructor wears the swordbelt with Winter Service 'B' uniform. (USMC A602465)

are used to 'dress up' the Embassy Guard's uniform. Other items of MP equipment may also be worn. Blue Dress 'D' is similar to 'C', but uses the quarter-length-sleeve khaki shirt without a tie. 'Blue Delta' is also authorised wear for ceremonies during hot weather.

B1: First Lieutenant, White Dress 'A', 1983

The White Dress Uniform for Marine officers dates back to 1912, and is virtually unchanged since then. When worn with medals (the 'A' Uniform, as here), no metal badges are worn. The hat's quatrefoil decoration is a traditional distinction for Marine officers and appears on all their hat covers. The white name tag, from a photograph, is a non-standard item, possibly authorised by a local command.

B2: Staff Sergeant, Blue-White Dress 'A', 1975

This is a Dress Uniform authorised for special events and ceremonies, for both officers and enlisted men. It is an 'organisational' uniform, i.e. not authorised for individual wear. It is created by wearing the blue tunic with white trousers and white hat cover. Swords for officers and NCOs may be prescribed, and enlisted ranks wear the white Dress Belt and Buckle. (This staff sergeant has the NCO pattern; below the grade of corporal, the Dress Buckle is plain.) The Blue-White uniform is usually worn by unit drill teams and colour guards, and these may, in turn, authorise special accessories. These might include a black Sam Browne belt for officers, white frogs and bayonet scabbards for enlisted men, and gold-plated (Hamilton Wash) buttons for all. Certain units with ceremonial duties in Washington have even been authorised to procure non-standard raincoats and overcoats so that the uniform may be worn during bad weather.

B3: Musician, US Marine Band, 1983

The United States Marine Band has carried out ceremonial functions in Washington since 1800. The variety and importance of its duties are reflected in the Dress Regulations, which devote an entire section to this unit. Some of the uniforms prescribed, such as those of the Director, Assistant Director and the Band's Drum Major, are among the most colourful ever worn in the American military. Ordinary Musicians, male and female, are also issued a variety of uniforms. The one illustrated is the Summer Full Dress Uniform with the red coat traditional for the Marine Band. The white trousers are summer issue, blue ones are worn in winter. No rank insignia are now worn with this uniform, although medals are permitted. Members of bands of other Marine commands wear the normal range of Dress Uniforms, with the addition of such Honor Guard equipment as may be prescribed by local authority.

C1: First Lieutenant, Winter Service 'A', 1983

This contemporary officer's uniform is virtually identical in style both to Marine enlisted uniforms, and to the Service Dress of World War II. The only changes for officers during this period were the dropping of the Sam Browne belt in 1942 and the change from brown accessories to black in 1963. However, during the post-war period, two other forms of Service Dress were worn. The Green Wool Service Jacket (see plate C2) was authorised from 1945–1968; and in 1957 a special version of the Service Coat was authorised for officers and staff NCOs. This had a bellows back, and was worn until the end of 1970. This officer wears Naval Aviator wings and the current (post-1958) type of Marksmanship Badges. With this system, only basic Rifle and Pistol badges are awarded in one of three categories: Expert, Sharpshooter and Marksman. Bars are added only to the Expert badges, and denote additional re-qualifications at the same level of proficiency. All Marines re-qualify with their basic weapons annually.

C2: Staff Sergeant, Winter Service 'A', 1954

This uniform had its origins in early 1943, when the veteran 1st Marine Division arrived in Australia for rest and re-equipment after Guadalcanal. Lacking any form of Service Uniform, the Marines were issued with Australian battledress. This proved extremely popular, and in 1944 it was decided to adopt it as a standard item for the Corps. (At the same time, in Europe, the US Army had adopted their own approximately similar 'Ike Jacket', based upon British battledress.) The Marine jacket was virtually identical to the Australian model, except that eyelets were provided in the open lapels to attach the 'globe and anchor' insignia, and green plastic buttons replaced the original tan ones. Designated the Green Wool Service Jacket, it was first issued in quantity to returning World War II veterans. It was issued in addition to the normal Service Coat until the early 1960s, and was finally abolished in 1968. Weapons Qualification Badges follow the 1937–58 system, with large badges for Rifle medals and small ones for Pistol awards; supplementary bars denoted qualification with additional types of weapons. The ribbons denote World War II and Korean War service.

C3: Staff Sergeant, Winter Service 'A', 1945

'Marine Green' was adopted for the Corps' Service

Women Marines touring Disneyland in 1966 in Green and White Summer Service Dress, with white gloves and black accessories. (USMC A230092)

The Director and Sergeant-Major of Women Marines arrive for an inspection at Camp Pendleton, California in 1971. All personnel wear the two-piece Green and White Summer Uniform; the inspection party wear the Green Summer Service Cap, with knotted white cords indicating officers or staff NCOs. The nervous lieutenant wears the Summer Service Garrison Cap. (USMC A355503)

Uniform in 1912, and the introduction of an open collar in 1928 brought the uniform to virtually its present form. During World War II, in an effort to conserve strategic metals, brown plastic was substituted for bronze in enlisted men's hat and collar devices. (Officers substituted sterling silver for lapel devices only.) The enlisted man's leather Garrison Belt was supplanted by a cloth type in 1943, but both types remained in use for the remainder of the war; indeed, the Garrison Belt was still issued as late as 1949 for some special guard duties. Early in World War II Army-style cloth shoulder patches were adopted by some elements of the Fleet Marine Force, Pacific; this sergeant wears the patch of the 6th Marine Division. The authority

for the practice seemed to be local unit orders; the Corps frowned upon the concept, and the patches officially disappeared from post-war uniforms in 1947. (The designs themselves remain as markings on vehicles, award certificates, signs, etc.) The peculiar chevrons worn by this NCO date from 1937, when a jumble of pre-war enlisted rank insignia was simplified into two main categories, distinguished by the use of either arcs or bars at the base of the insignia. The bars here denote a staff NCO, e.g. one in the Quartermaster or Pay Department, rather than holding a Line position in the same grade. The 1937 system was still a bit too complicated and, in 1946, the Marines dropped all their traditional NCO titles and adopted those of the Army.

D1: Lieutenant-Colonel, Summer Service 'A', 1956
The first khaki summer uniforms were adopted by the Marine Corps at the time of the Spanish-American War. The officer's version changed little

between 1928 and its abolition at the end of 1976. Only the abandonment of the Sam Browne belt in 1942, and the change in leather colour in 1963, affected it. This officer's ribbons indicate participation in several World War II campaigns, postwar duties in Japan and North China, and service in Korea.

D2: Corporal, Summer Service 'B', 1961
Marines started wearing khaki for summer during the Spanish-American War, but the shirt and trouser combination as Service Dress dates only from 1938. As with many Marine uniforms, there were versions in different fabrics: in this case, tropical worsted and cotton. The khaki shirt and trousers were worn as the standard enlisted summer uniform until the early 1970s, with virtually no changes in appearance. This was also authorised wear for officers (their Summer 'C') during that period. The 'globe and anchor' device was worn on enlisted men's shirt collars only between 1952 and 1961. The width of the tie changed several times— oddly enough, almost in opposition to civilian fashions: wide ties were prescribed when narrow ones were 'in', and vice-versa. The tie-clip is the pattern for enlisted men; a different version is worn by officers and staff NCOs. Most commonly, the uniform was worn with the khaki Garrison Cap, but the Service Hat with khaki cover was also worn. Badges and ribbons were optional. It might also be mentioned that staff NCOs are authorised to purchase and wear officer-quality uniforms if they wish.

D3: Drill Instructor, Summer Service 'C', 1983
All the American armed forces introduced lightweight synthetic fabrics for their Service Uniforms in the early 1960s. A decade later this would bring about a radical change in the appearance of Service Dress. The woollen winter uniforms were replaced by lighter weight versions which could be worn all year round. Specialised Summer Dress also disappeared: in summer, troops would now wear a shirt and trousers version of the winter uniform. For the Marine Corps the change was less radical than for some of the other services, but it meant the end of

the all-khaki uniform in 1976. This Marine Drill Instructor wears green polyester/rayon wash-and-wear trousers with the quarter-length-sleeve khaki shirt, introduced in 1960. The Campaign Hat, a symbol of the 'Old Corps' dropped in 1942, was re-instated in early 1961 for Drill Instructors and

Korean War Marine rifleman, in M1944 utilities, World War II-type camouflage helmet cover and web leggings, M1941 Haversack worn as Light Marching Pack, and extra ammunition bandoliers. (USMC 53235)

SUSPENDER STRAP KEEPER

BLANKET ROLL STRAP

BAYONET ATTACHMENT

SUSPENDER STRAP KEEPER

ENTRENCHING TOOL ATTACHMENT

FLAP

FLAP STRAP BUCKLE

BAYONET LOOP

SUSPENDER STRAP

ENTRENCHING TOOL STRAP

COUPLING

SUSPENDER STRAP

COUPLING

PACK STRAP LOOP

PACK STRAP LOOP

BELT SUPPORTING STRAP

FLAP STRAPS

7.1 The haversack.

7.3 The marching pack.

7.4 The field marching pack.

7.5 The transport pack.

7.6 The field transport pack.

COUPLING STRAP

FLAP STRAP BUCKLE

COUPLING STRAP BUCKLE

FLAP STRAP

PACK STRAP LOOPS

7.2 The knapsack.

members of Marine shooting teams. The non-commissioned officer's sword is only worn for ceremonies, but the Senior DI of each recruit platoon will also wear the swordbelt alone as a symbol of his status. The other DIs wear the Pistol Belt during training.

E1: First Lieutenant, Winter Service 'A', 1952
Women have been part of the Marine Corps continuously since 1943 and, before that, served briefly with them in World War I. Changes in women's uniforms since 1945 have been at least as complex as those for male Marines. Affected by civilian fashions, praticality and even changing concepts of a woman's rôle in the military, Woman Marines have still managed to retain certain traditional features in all their uniforms. This is especially true of Service Dress. This woman officer wears the 1952 (M-52) Winter Service Uniform, one of the new series introduced that year. The World War II uniform it replaced was similar, but the older Jacket had a different pocket arrangement and the male Service Tie was worn. In basic style, this uniform has changed little over the years. As with men's Service Dress, only rank insignia differentiates officer and enlisted ranks. Skirt length has varied with prevalent fashion, but the hat is virtually identical to that adopted in 1943. The purse and dress pumps with bows were a World War II issue which seem to have persisted into the early 1950s. Thereafter, dress shoes were purchased privately. The 1963 leather colour change also affected Woman Marines, requiring a new purse among other items. At the present time all women's uniforms are under review, but the current Service Dress is still an obvious descendant of the M-52 uniform shown here. In style, a green necktab has replaced the ascot tie. As with the man's Service Uniform, there is now also a lightweight version for year-round wear. An optional woman's beret in Marine Green was briefly authorised in the late 1970s, but dropped in 1981.

The Marine M1941 Pack System, comprising Haversack, Knapsack and Belt Suspenders, was used from 1942 until the end of the 1970s. It could be made up in the four ways shown; or the Haversack alone could be worn as a knapsack-style pack— the Light Marching Pack, not shown here. (Guidebook for Marines, 1954 ed.)

40

E2: Sergeant, Summer Service Dress, 1960
Women's summer uniforms have undergone the most changes since World War II. The one shown was worn between 1952 and 1969, originally supplanting several of World War II vintage. It was replaced in its turn in the mid-1960s by a two-piece Jacket and Skirt in the same material. Currently a lightweight version of the Winter Uniform is worn, or a skirt and blouse combination based on it. Slacks may be prescribed for certain duties. As with male Summer Service Dress, the uniforms of officers and enlisted grades are identical except for insignia.

E3: Sergeant, Blue Dress 'B', 1966
Blue Dress for women was introduced with the M-52 series uniforms. Separate versions were designed for officers and enlisted grades. Both types were essentially feminine equivalents of corresponding male uniforms, the officer's jacket being made in darker blue, untrimmed, with pointed cuffs, etc. However, since a lighter coloured skirt was considered unflattering to most women, no attempt was made to copy the 'two-tone' look of the male uniform: skirts would match the jackets in colour. The enlisted woman's uniform, shown here, circa 1966, remained unchanged in style from roughly 1952 to the present. Its details also reflect the men's uniform, e.g. in trim and cuff style. The hat is a blue version of the women's Service Hat; it is worn by all enlisted grades and officers of the rank of captain and below. (Majors and above wear gold cords and oakleaf decoration on the visor.) For formal occasions, charcoal-grey stockings are worn. While this version of the Blue uniform is still in use, a newer uniform is being phased in. One reason for the change is the expanded rôle of women in the armed forces. With their presence at so many mixed formations, it was felt necessary to bring their uniforms more into conformity with the men's to present a tidier appearance. A second motive was to update the uniform in line with current civilian fashions, where slacks are now permitted business attire for women. For the moment, however, it has been decided that the uniform will only be worn with the skirt.

F1: Tank Commander, Korea, summer 1950
This Marine officer wears the later, M1944 pattern utilities, also worn as Summer Combat Dress in Korea. These had some odd features. The trousers had only three pockets: two side cargo pockets, and a single large horizontal 'seat' pocket at the rear. Each closed by a flap and two visible buttons. In addition to its single breast pocket, the jacket had two flat map pockets concealed beneath the front. As with the M1942 utilities, the jacket could be worn either loose, or tucked into the pants. Tankers wore the World War II Composition Helmet with M1944 Dust Goggles. A .45 pistol is worn with Shoulder Holster M7, the M1936 Pistol Belt, two-pocket .45 ammunition pouch and M1942 Field Dressing Pouch. Officer's rank insignia was sometimes worn, but more often removed in the field or worn beneath the lapel. Tankers often tucked utility trousers inside sock tops to keep them out of the way. The World War II 'boondocker' field boots, made in 'rough-side-out' leather, were standard issue for most of the Korean War.

F2: Machine gunner, Korea, summer 1950
In addition to the weight of his weapon (.30cal. Browning M1919A4 MMG), this Marine also

Navy Corpsman treating a wounded civilian in Korea, August 1950, displays the curious large rear seat pocket of the M1944 utilities; the author has been unable to discover the intended purpose of this. (USMC A01349)

carries his Combat Pack (M1941 Haversack worn as Light Marching Pack), M1943 Entrenching Tool, bedroll and sleeping bag. Several of his other accoutrements are unique to the Marine Corps. The canteen cover with cross-over flaps is a USMC item from World War II. The Jungle First Aid Pouch was developed by the Army, but then dropped by them in 1945; the Marines, however, retained it up to the present day, now in a much up-dated version. Likewise, the Grenade Pouch (which came in one-, two-, and three-pocket versions) was an Army item retained by the Marines into the 1960s. As a machine gunner, this man also carries a .45 pistol in M1916 Holster. The uncomfortable leggings were often discarded in combat, but not before the NKPA nicknamed the Marines 'Yellow-legs'. An extra camouflage shelter half is worn beneath the packstraps.

F3: Rifleman, Korea, summer 1950
The Marines issued two types of World War II utilities as summer combat dress in Korea. This rifleman wears the M1942 pattern, made in cotton HBT (Herringbone Twill) material. The three-pocket jacket could be worn loose, as shown, or tucked into the trousers like a shirt. Personal equipment comprises the M1936 ten-pocket Cart-ridge Belt (each pocket holding one eight-round

'enbloc' clip for the M1 Garand), M1 Bayonet in Scabbard M7, Jungle First Aid Pouch and M1941 Pack and Belt Suspenders. Additional ammunition is carried in a six-pocket cotton bandolier. The canvas leggings and helmet camouflage cover were unique to the Marine Corps in 1950. The crude hand-marking of rank insignia is a continuation of a World War II practice, unsatisfactory even at the time.

G1: Rifleman, Korea, winter 1950–53
Winter Combat Dress, for most of the war, was based on the 'layering' principle, with a variety of garments worn one over the other. Typically, these might include woollen underwear, wool shirt and trousers, sweater, field jacket with liner, and the alpaca-lined, parka-type Overcoat shown here. The parka's hood was supposed to fit over the helmet, but most people wore it as shown. The canvas and rubber 'shoepacs' created problems for the wearer: they made the feet sweat with any activity, then allowed moisture to freeze inside. Trigger-finger shell mittens, worn over wool glove inserts, protected the hands. Towards the end of the war a new range of winter clothing was introduced, replacing the items shown. The M1951 System remains in use to the present.

G2: Officer, Korea, spring 1951
This company officer wears an M1943 Field Jacket with liner over his utility uniform, probably with a sweater underneath. His wool scarf and fur cap are

Preparations for a patrol in Korea, June 1952. The Marines at centre and right wear the M1937 Magazine Belt for the BAR, a popular weapon. In this case the webbing gear is worn over the M1951 Armor Vest—an awkward arrangement, but it allowed the whole load to be shucked off in one go. (USMC A162602)

UN winter issue. He is armed with the .30cal. carbine M2, with 30-round magazine. This weapon established a mixed reputation in Korea: its fully-automatic option and light weight made it initially popular, but it proved prone to jamming, especially in winter. Further 15-round magazines are carried in a pouch on the stock. The officer's .45 is worn on the Pistol Belt together with its magazine pouch, and the M4 Bayonet in Scabbard M8. A compass case is attached below the Jungle First Aid Pouch. The M1943 Combat Boots are not Marine issue, but privately obtained from the Army.

G3: Automatic Rifleman, Korea, 1953
The Army and Marine Corps conducted joint research into body armour in the summer and fall of 1951, but chose different solutions to the problem. The original Marine M1951 Armor Vest (not to be confused with the different Army type designated M1952) was issued in the spring of 1952. There were several variants; this version, with asymmetrical front closure and breast pocket, is a later type (and drawn from one actually marked 'M1952'). The Army, having development problems with its own body armour, procured 63,000 Marine vests as

Admiral John S. McCain, Jr, inspects personnel of the 1st Reconnaissance Battalion in Vietnam, December 1969. The men wear M1956 equipment over camouflage utilities with 'boonie hats'. The man at extreme right also carries a Unit 1 Medical Bag on his chest. (USMC A372452)

an interim measure in 1952. The Armored Groin Protector was also issued. It seemed useful during the later, positional phase of the Korean fighting, but eventually proved too awkward for more active situations. This Marine carries the rugged and dependable BAR, the Browning Automatic Rifle M1918A2. Twelve of its 20-round magazines are carried in pockets of the M1937 BAR Belt. Although the M26 hand grenade was introduced in 1953, this man carries the older Mk II type. The Marine boot differed in several features from the Army boot of the period. It was made in 'rough-side-out' leather, and had 'speedlace' metal pegs instead of eyelets above the instep.

H1: Force Recon, Camp Lejeune, 1955
In the 1950s the Marines decided they had a need for intelligence gathering beyond the normal tactical level. Their response was the establishment of special units reporting directly to the Fleet Marine Force commanders, Atlantic and Pacific.

Marines of Co.M, 3/4, on 'search and clear' operations near Phu Bai in July 1965. Note 'assault slings' adapted from the standard M-14 rifle issue. (USMC A184988)

The units would have both parachute and scuba capability. This man wears the World War II reversible M1944 camouflage uniform of shirt and trousers, usually called 'the Raider Uniform'. The jacket shared certain features with the contemporary M1944 Utility type—the two concealed map pockets, for example. A headscarf has been improvised for a helmet camouflage cover. While combat boots were usually worn, for some types of operations a lighter shoe was preferred. In addition to the M3A1 'Grease Gun' shown, the ordinary range of infantry weapons was employed. The Kabar knife has been a Marine tradition since World War II, and is usually issued to anyone whose primary weapon does not take a bayonet.

H2: Sergeant, Lebanon, 1958
As they always do, the Marines made the 1958 landing in Lebanon in full combat order. This NCO, taken from a photograph, wears the newly issued M1955 Armor Vest. As compared to the previous M1952, it had a different, 'standard' front closure, and added a very useful rope ridge to the right side, to retain a slung rifle on the march. A reinforced and eyeletted band at the waist allowed equipment with M1910 horizontal hook fasteners to be attached. This NCO's pistol holster, M1910 field dressing pouch, canteen and bayonet are so carried. (In practice, the continual banging and flapping of loose equipment made the idea impractical, and few Marines bothered much with the feature.) The sergeant's pack and blanket roll are worn secured to a World War II packboard, which allowed more items to be carried comfortably.

H3: Officer, 1958
At the end of the Korean War a new utility uniform was introduced into service. There were two versions, one made in HBT cloth and a later type made in ordinary heavy twill. Both were worn interchangeably. The jacket had a concealed map pocket located inside on the left side. The khaki belt and frame buckle have been Marine trademarks since World War II, and are still worn. The characteristic utility cap (called a 'cover' as are all

Marine headgear) is a Marine development of a World War II item once issued to both Army and Marine Corps. (The Army stopped wearing theirs during Korea.) Originally it was developed from a cap worn by civilian railroad workers. Officers wear pin-on rank insignia in the field, on both lapels and, optionally, on the cap.

I1: Sergeant, 1st Marine Recon Battalion; Vietnam, 1966
Initially, Marine Recon personnel wore standard utility uniforms in Vietnam. By 1966, however, locally-made camouflage uniforms were available. This NCO wears a set of the famous 'tiger-stripe' pattern, together with Vietnamese-made jungle boots (called 'Bata boots' after the principal manufacturer). A beret was the mark of élite forces in Vietnam, and Marine Recon personnel wore either a black or a tiger-stripe type. The weapon is a Stoner 63, which the Marines tested in the early 1960s. The Corps was very impressed with the Stoner System, in which a series of components could be made up into several types of assault rifles or light machine guns. At one time the Corps attempted to adopt it, but were overruled. Nevertheless, a number of the weapons were issued to special units in Vietnam, where they established a mixed reputation. In its LMG configuration, the Stoner used ammunition in several forms. Thirty-round magazines are carried in an M1937 BAR Belt, and the ammo can with linked 5.56mm belt is carried in a scrounged Unit 1 Medical Bag. Like many Marines, this man has acquired Army issue M1956 Belt Suspenders to replace his uncomfortable Marine type. A Kabar knife is worn attached to one strap. The standard Combat Pack is used, with an M1944 Machete carried at the side.

I2: Rifleman, Vietnam, 1965
When Secretary of Defense Robert MacNamara took office in 1961, he decided to reduce the number of common items in use by the different services. Starting in 1962, the Army OG 107 utility uniform began to be issued to Marines: it would take many years to completely replace the older type utilities. The black Army Combat Boots replaced the brown Marine type at the same time. The adoption of the M-14 Rifle and M-6 Bayonet also brought changes to Marine equipment. The M1961 Rifle Belt and Pouches (each pouch holding one 20-round

Two brothers, both assigned to Danang, illustrate Marine utility uniforms in early 1969. The man on the left still wears the OG 107 issue; his brother on the right, a mixture of standard jungle and camouflage utilities. (USMC)

magazine) were introduced, still worn with M1941 Belt Suspenders, M1910 canteens, Jungle First Aid Pouch and the Marine Pack. A new pattern camouflage Shelter Half was used alongside World War II and plain OD Army types, never replacing either. The World War II Grenade Pouches were still in use, since the Marine web gear made no other provision for carrying grenades. The M-14 Rifle was convertible to fully automatic fire (the decision for this was made at battalion level) and the bipod was an optional feature if this was done. A helmet camouflage retaining band has been improvised from an old rubber inner tube. Starting at the end of the Korean War, enlisted Marines began wearing metal pin-on rank devices on the collars of combat clothing—an idea eventually adopted by the Army as well.

I3: Grenadier, Vietnam, 1966
The M-79 40mm Grenade Launcher was another

Presenting a very different picture from the 3/4 Marines in summer 1965—see earlier photo—these personnel of the 3rd Marine Regt. wait for helicopters during Operation 'Taylor Common' in December 1968; one sports a small American flag. Note the Army rucksacks, and the C-ration box at right. (USMC A192410)

new weapon introduced in Vietnam. Its rounds were issued in cotton bandoliers, each holding six rounds in two plastic 'packs'. Originally two of these bandoliers were standard issue, but grenadiers soon learned simply to take as many as possible. A .45 pistol and Kabar knife were also carried. In addition to his own load, this man has been given two 7.62 ammo boxes to carry. With his pack, entrenching tool and hand grenade pouch (this time, a 'two'), they are strapped to a World War II packboard. A green nylon rain poncho with liner is carefully folded beneath the packstraps. The M-17 Protective Mask was often used on operations—contrary to popular opinion at the time, both the US and North Vietnamese made use of CS gas in combat. Since the carrying capacity of the Marine Pack was so limited (the Army M1956 Pack was no better), this Marine has been forced to stuff his C-Ration cans into extra socks and drape these about his person as necessary. The utility jacket is discarded, and trousers are worn unbloused in the hot climate. A towel is worn around the neck as a sweatrag. The 'brown side' of the helmet cover was sometimes more useful than the 'green', particularly in some coastal regions. Green T-shirts appeared in about 1966.

J1: Machine gunner, Vietnam, 1967
Together with other American troops in Vietnam, the Marines began to receive their first issues of jungle utilities in early 1966. There were several slightly different patterns (see MAA 143, *Armies of the Vietnam War (2)*). A special type of jungle boot was also developed and issued; among other things, it offered protection to the foot from enemy 'punji stake' foot traps. By this time the M1955 Armor Vest had been modified by the addition of two front pockets. Details varied from unit to unit; unmodified examples of the vest also continued in use. As a machine gunner, this man is also armed with a .45 pistol. The carrying of the Kabar knife, wedged behind the holster, is typical. Ammunition belts for the 7.62mm M-60 machine gun are worn bandolier-fashion. An extra field dressing and a toothbrush for weapons' cleaning are stuck in the helmet band, this time an Army issue type. Many Marine units required the individual to write his name and serial number on the helmet's camouflage cover. Most Marines added further

comments, personal mottos, hometowns, and the inevitable 'short-timer's' calendar—one month longer than his Army counterpart's, since the Marines served 13-month combat tours while the 'doggies' went home in twelve.

J2: Rifleman, Vietnam, 1970
Camouflage jungle utilities were introduced in Vietnam in late 1967, initially only to élite units (Army Special Forces and LRRPs, Navy SEALs, Marine Recon, etc.). However, in late 1968 the Marine Corps decided to procure them for all their personnel in-country. The change took some time, but was virtually complete by the end of 1969. The matching wide-brimmed hat was seen alongside standard utility 'covers' or personally-acquired camouflage equivalents—as here. M-16 rifle was introduced in 1966, often so quickly that some units did not initially receive its companion M-6 Bayonet.

CH-46 helicopter door gunner in Vietnam, 1967; he wears CS/FRP-1 coveralls, APH-6A Pilot's Helmet, OD T-shirt and B-3 gloves. (USMC)

Marine CH-46 helicopter crews in current SPH-3 helmets, ceramic aircrew armour vests and CWU-27 flight suits. Aircrew are required to apply reflective tape to their helmets, and a wide latitude is permitted in designs: the result is a rainbow of gaudy patterns. (USMC)

The M-16's 20-round magazines were not especially compatible with the M1961 pouches, and many Marines, such as this man, acquired the superior M1956 Army type. The Army belt suspenders, more comfortable than the Marine issue, were also a popular item. In addition to capacity and comfort, the Army equipment permitted the safe carrying of grenades, something that often had to be improvised with the Marine web gear. The OD plastic canteen and helmet band are also Army issue. By 1970 many Marines in-country had solved the pack problem by discarding the issue item and acquiring a superior one from the Army or the ARVN. Even North Vietnamese packs were pressed into service. This man has the standard Army Lightweight Tropical Rucksack, with frame.

J3: Helicopter Crewman, Vietnam, 1969
During the Vietnam War, Marine helicopter crews wore the same flying clothing as fixed-wing personnel: in this case, the CS/FRP-1 polyanamide fire-resistant coveralls, first issued in 1967. The SPH-3 Flying Helmet, especially developed for helicopter crews, was introduced in 1969; prior to its

ONTOS M50A1 of the 1st Anti-Tank Bn. at Chu Lai in May 1966. Not a particularly successful vehicle, it came into its own during the Hue street fighting of Tet 1968, when its 106mm recoilless rifles proved devastating in direct support of infantry. The crewmen wear standard utilities and CVC (Combat Vehicle Crewman's) helmets. (USMC A369167)

introduction, older models of jet pilot's helmets were worn. The need for some kind of protective armour for helicopter crews was recognised early in the war. Ground troops' body armour was worn as an interim measure; specialised armour for helicopter crewmen appeared in 1966. This version is a later type (distinguished by the pocket), meant for crew chiefs and door gunners, whose tasks required them to move around the aircraft. Another version existed for pilots, who had armoured seats to sit in; this lacked the rear plate. The armour itself was much heavier and more cumbersome than that issued to ground troops. As personal protection this man carries an issue .38cal. Smith & Wesson Model 10 revolver in a private purchase holster. His M1936 Pistol Belt has been rigger-modified with cartridge loops. A Kabar knife is also carried.

K1: Grenadier, Lebanon, 1983

This Marine wears the latest, possibly the last variant of the M-1 helmet, with LC-1 suspension. The 'woodland' camouflage cover was introduced in the early 1970s. Over his BDUs he wears the new PASGT (Personal Armor System, Ground Troops) vest, which is replacing the older M1955 pattern. It is made of Kevlar, which has bullet-resistant properties; previous vests protected only against shrapnel. A helmet made of the same material, dubbed the 'Fritz' because of its Germanic shape, is being procured in 1984. The pack and LC-1 equipment together comprise the ALICE (All-Purpose Individual Combat Equipment) set, now in use by all US forces. The flat object attached to the pack is the carrier for a folding entrenching tool. The M203, a development of a Vietnam-era weapon, combines a 40mm grenade launcher with the M-16 Rifle.

K2: Recon Marine, FMF-Atlantic; Camp Lejeune, 1983

In the early 1980s the Army, Air Force and Marines adopted a new camouflage combat uniform. It was made in a half-and-half nylon-cotton mix, designed for maximum burn protection. Designated the BDU, for Battledress Uniform, it uses the 'woodland' colours, but with individual camouflage segments 1.6 times as large. The dyes are also specially treated to reduce infra-red signature. The USMC decal is not used with this uniform. Other changes include a larger collar and smaller,

Marines of 32nd MAU watch equipment off-loaded from a Navy LST in 'the Root', September 1982, when they arrived to resume duties at the International Airport. Note 'woodland' camouflage uniform, PASGT armour vests, and LC-1 equipment; the man at the right's new nylon Jungle First Aid Kit shows well on the back of his belt.

unpleated pockets. Only Recon Marines use the Ranger-type hat. The DMS boots were introduced in the 1970s. Personal equipment is the LC-2 pattern, of nylon Pistol Belt, 30-Round Magazine Pouches, 'Y' Belt Suspenders, etc. An M-17 Protective Mask is worn at the hip. The Heckler & Koch MP5 SD3 is one of two silenced weapons available to recon units; the Ingram MAC-11 is the other.

K3: Armour Crewman, 1983

In the late 1970s the Marines decided to adopt a camouflage utility uniform for year-round wear, world wide. The uniforms themselves were taken from Vietnam-era stocks, and came in two camouflage schemes: the original 'leaf-pattern' colours, and a later 'woodland' scheme. The Vietnam type had slanted jacket pockets, but the post-war production replaced these with a smaller, squarer type. The Marine supply system did not distinguish between any of these, and all remain in use to the present day, with the square-pocket 'woodland' pattern gradually predominating. While subdued T-shirts are sometimes issued, the white version is still very much in evidence. After some discussion, it was decided to keep the Marine utility cap, but in 'woodland' colours. Jungle boots are still occasionally issued in warm climates from declining Vietnam stocks. As an armoured vehicle crewman, this corporal carries the current DH-132 CVC (Combat Vehicle Crewman) Helmet, also painted in 'woodland' colours at the unit level. The American flag patch came into vogue in the early 1980s for overseas deployments.

L1: F4U Corsair Pilot, VMF-214; Korea, 1950
In general, since 1945, the Marines have used the same flying clothing as the Navy, and their equipment is provided directly by their sister service. The F4U Corsair was originally designed in World War II as a high-performance fighter, but by Korea it was well into a second career as a close-support attack 'plane; it performed outstanding service throughout the war. The figure wears the

The ALICE web gear worn over the PASGT by a 32nd MAU engineer. Note 'Y' configuration of Belt Suspenders. The device in his trouser pocket is part of the Wurlitzer mine detector. (USMC)

standard Navy flying dress of the period, Z-2 Anti-G Coveralls and Navy Deck Shoes. His BuAer (Bureau of Aeronautics) Mark 2 Life Preserver was introduced in about 1948. Attached are a Distress Light Signal (which came with green, red or clear covers), a private purchase PAL RH-36 Knife, and the issue .38 revolver (S&W Military & Police, or Colt Victory Model). A package of shark repellant is also attached, ready for immediate use. His Gentex H-4 Flying Helmet, introduced in 1948, is worn with M-1944 Navy Flying Goggles. The helmet's communications system is contained in an inner flying cap donned separately before putting on the helmet. A boom microphone was used at low altitudes, with a second microphone contained within the MS-22001 Oxygen Mask. World War II-era Summerweight Flying Gloves are worn. VMF-214, famous as Col. 'Pappy' Boyington's 'Black Sheep' in World War II, was among the first Corsair squadrons sent to Korea.

L2: F-8 Crusader Pilot, VMF(AW)-235; Vietnam, 1966
The F-8 Crusader was the last Navy fighter to use cannon as primary armament, and its pilots proudly proclaimed themselves 'the last of the gunfighters'. En route to Vietnam in 1965, Marine Fighter Squadron VMF-235 arranged for the purchase in Japan of camouflage flight suits for all of its flying personnel: the material used was a 'tiger-stripe' pattern originally intended for the Japanese Self-Defence Forces. (The use of custom flight suits was done away with in 1967, with the introduction of fire-resistant materials.) In Vietnam, Escape and Evasion (E&E) was a major consideration, and Jungle Boots were preferred by many pilots. Flying equipment includes a Z-4 Anti-G Suit, MA-2 Torso Harness and Mk-3C Life Preserver. The APH-6D Helmet is worn with A-13A Oxygen Mask. Survival equipment—flares, radio, E&E Kit, emergency ammunition, rations and water—is contained within the SV-1 Survival Vest. A survival knife is carried, and the pilot is also armed with a .38cal. S&W Model 10 revolver and some 50 rounds of ammunition. The helmet bag is a custom model in green leather; and the kneeboard MXU-P is turned to the aircraft's preflight checklist procedures. The B-3A Summer Flying Gloves are a World War II Air Force model, adopted post-war by the Navy and Marines and still in use.

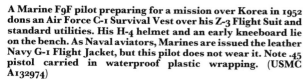

A Marine F9F pilot preparing for a mission over Korea in 1952 dons an Air Force C-1 Survival Vest over his Z-3 Flight Suit and standard utilities. His H-4 helmet and an early kneeboard lie on the bench. As Naval aviators, Marines are issued the leather Navy G-1 Flight Jacket, but this pilot does not wear it. Note .45 pistol carried in waterproof plastic wrapping. (USMC A132974)

Flying dress for a 1st MAW fighter pilot in Vietnam, 1967, includes CS/FRP-1 Coveralls, brown flying boots, and B-3A Gloves. Equipment includes the Z-4 Anti-G Suit, cutaway MA-2 Torso Harness, Mk.2 Life Preserver, and APH-6D Helmet. The SV-1 Survival Vest has been modified to include a pocket for a shroud-cutter, knife and radio. The pilot carries the RSSK-1 Seat Pack Survival Kit from his aircraft. (USMC A421962)

L3: AV-8A Harrier pilot, VMA-231, 1976

The Marines became interested in the Harrier VSTOL fighter in the early 1970s. With the reduction of the Navy's carrier fleet, the Marines felt that they could not rely on the continual presence of a carrier to support future amphibious operations. What was needed was a close-support aircraft of their own, which could be rapidly put ashore to support ground operations. It would also have to operate under relatively primitive conditions, something the British had designed the Harrier to do. The Harrier could also fly from amphibious landing ships, and provide a limited air defence capability. The first Marine pilots to receive the Harrier wore the complete British flying

equipment that came with the aircraft. Gradually the more familiar American equipment was adapted to the Harrier's systems and, by 1977, a mixture of the two had become standard. This pilot wears the current CWU-27 Summer Flying Coveralls and Safety-Toe Flying Boots. The cigarette/pen pocket has been rigger-modified with a flap to prevent the ingestion of loose items into engines. His APH-6D Helmet has been fitted with a modified visor for better upwards visibility; it is worn with Oxygen Mask A-13A. His flying equipment includes a modified cutaway MA-2 Torso Harness and Mk. II Gravity Suit. Survival gear includes a Light Distress Marker SDU-5/E and a British Mk 17 Life Preserver.

Notes sur les planches en couleur

A1, A2 Remarquez les légères différences de la version officier et de la version sous-officier de cet uniforme de cérémonie et les différences des uniformes 1950 et 1970. Seul un revêtement de chapeau blanc est porté depuis 1957; les articles en cuir, qui étaient bruns sont devenus noirs en 1963. Les galons situés sous les chevrons du sous-officier indiquent deux engagements de quatre ans. **A3** Version portée en été pour les services de cérémonie sur les bases militaires.

B1 Cet uniforme, réservé aux officiers, n'a pratiquement pas changé depuis 1912. **B2** Cette combinaison des uniformes de cérémonie bleus et blancs n'est portée que par des groupes tels que les équipes de démonstration de l'exercice et les gardes d'honneur. **B3** Uniforme de cérémonie d'été pour l'orchestre; des pantalons bleus sont portés en hiver.

C1 Cet uniforme est très similaire à celui des troupes et à la tenue de service de la deuxième guerre mondiale. **C2** Cet uniforme était copié sur l'uniforme australien réglementaire pour la Première Division des Marines en Australie en 1943. **C3** Presque inchangé depuis 1928, date à laquelle apparut le col ouvert, cet uniforme '*Marine green*' a des chevrons du modèle 1937. Les écussons d'épaule d'unité—ici la sixième Division de Marines—disparurent en 1947.

D1 Il y a eu peu de changements dans cet uniforme d'été entre 1928 et 1976, date à laquelle il fut aboli. **D2** Les insignes du col ne furent portés qu'entre 1952 et 1961 sur cet uniforme d'été pour les troupes. **D3** L'uniforme entièrement kaki disparut en 1976, remplacé par cette combinaison. Le chapeau à larges bords et la ceinture d'épée sont des caractéristiques particulières des instructeurs d'exercices.

E1 Uniforme introduit en 1952; seuls les insignes de rang distinguent le modèle des officiers de celui des troupes. **E2** Uniforme porté entre 1952 et 1969. **E3** Modèle féminin de l'uniforme *Dress Blues* pour hommes, mais en un seul ton—on a estimé qu'un uniforme en deux tons ne serait pas flatteur. Il est demeuré essentiellement inchangé de 1952 à l'heure actuelle.

F1 '*Utilities*' de modèle 1944; le reste de cette tenue remonte aussi à la deuxième guerre mondiale. **F2** Mitrailleur, possédant un pistolet automatique comme arme personnelle. Cet équipement était appelé *Light Marching Pack*. **F3** Uniforme 1942 *HBT 'utility'* porté avec des équipements de la deuxième guerre mondiale. En 1950, les jambières en toile et le revêtement de camouflage du casque n'étaient plus portés que par les Marines.

G1 Le capuchon de la parka était supposé s'adapter au-dessus du casque mais il était généralement porté ainsi. Les couvre-chaussures en caoutchouc et en toile provoquaient des problèmes de condensation, laissant la sueur se geler à l'intérieur de la chaussure. **G2** Veste de campagne 1943 portée avec une doublure chaude et par dessus un chandail. A part le chapeau doublé de fourrure, ce personnage pourrait dater de la deuxième guerre mondiale. **G3** Le premier gilet pare-balles distribué aux troupes américaines était du modèle Marine M1951 illustré ici, distribué au printemps 1952. Le BAR fut très utilisé en Corée; 12 chargeurs sont transportés dans la ceinture spéciale.

H1 Ces unités spéciales de renseignement étaient directement responsables devant la *Fleet Marine Force Atlantic* et *Pacific*. L'uniforme de camouflage de la deuxième guerre mondiale fut repris pour ces spécialistes du parachutage et de la plongée sous-marine. **H2** Le gilet pare-balles M1955 avait des œillets à la partie inférieure pour la fixation de matériel; en fait, le balancement de tous ces articles était si gauche que peu d'hommes utilisaient ces œillets. **H3** Ce béret appartient en propre aux Marines depuis la guerre de Corée, durant laquelle il était également porté par les troupes de l'armée.

I1 Un uniforme de camouflage 'à rayures de tigre' fabriqué localement et des bottes de jungle vietnamiennes furent acquis pour remplacer les uniformes '*utility*' normalisés. Les hommes de *Recon Battalion* portaient des bérets soit noirs soit 'à rayures de tigre'. L'arme est le Stoner 63, utilisé par certaines unités spéciales. **I2** Tenue de combat OG107 du modèle armée, équipement de ceinture M1961 et le fusil M-14 étaient typiques des premières années de la guerre au Vietnam. **I3** Ce soldat, armé d'un lance-grenades M-79, porte le masque à gaz M-17; les troupes américaines et celles du Vietnam du Nord utilisaient des gaz durant le combat. Les rations glissées dans les chaussettes supplémentaires rappellent la médiocre capacité des havresacs des Marines. Deux boîtes de munitions sont fixées, avec son équipement personnel, à un *packboard* de la deuxième guerre mondiale.

J1 Les '*utilities*' de jungle commencèrent à apparaître en 1966. Le gilet pare-balles M1955 est modifié par l'addition de poches. La mitrailleuse M-60 est portée, ainsi qu'une ceinture pour réserve de munitions et un revolver personnel. **J2** A la fin de 1968, il fut décidé d'acquérir des uniformes de camouflage pour tous les Marines se trouvant au Vietnam, quoique leur distribution prit un certain temps. L'aspect du fusil M-16 rendit pratique l'acquisition de cartouchières M1956 de l'armée. **J3** Ce pilote porte une combinaison CS/FRP-1 ignifugée et le casque SPH-3, ainsi que le gilet pare-balles lourd spécial des équipes d'hélicoptères.

K1 Le nouveau gilet pare-balles Kevlar PASGT vu ici avec l'équipement 'ALICE' et le fusil/lance-grenades M203. **K2** Le nouvel uniforme de combat BDU en couleurs 'forêt', porté avec un équipement LC-2; Le H & K MP-5 est l'une des deux armes silencieuses—l'autre étant le Ingram—utilisée par les Marines de reconnaissance. **K3** Des '*utilities*' de camouflage sont portées par les Marines depuis la fin des années 1970. Les modèles 'feuilles' et les modèles 'forêt' ont tous deux été vus à mesure de l'épuisement des stocks 'feuilles'. Le casque de ce membre de l'équipe d'un véhicule blindé DH-132 est peint pour s'assortir à la tenue de camouflage.

L Les Marines pilotes ont généralement utilisé l'équipement et la tenue de vol de la Marine américaine. Les légendes en anglais de cette illustration donnent les noms techniques complets de tous les articles présentés et elles ne peuvent pas être traduites de façon utile.

Farbtafeln

A1, A2 Beachten Sie die kleinen Unterschiede an diesen Festuniformen von Offizieren und Unteroffizieren sowie die Unterschiede zwischen Uniformen von 1950 und 1970. Seit 1957 trug man lediglich einen weissen Hut. Vor 1963 waren Gegenstände aus Leder braun, danach schwarz. Die Streifen unter den Rankwinkeln der Unteroffiziers zeigen an, dass er sich auf vier Jahre verpflichtet hat. **A3** Eine Version, die man im Sommer bei zeremoniellen Anlässen auf militärischen Stützpunkten trägt.

B1 Diese Uniform, die nur Offiziere tragen, hat sich seit 1912 kaum geändert. **B2** Lediglich Gruppen wie Drillvorführteams oder die Ehrengarde tragen diese Kombination aus blauer und weisser Festuniform. **B3** Sommer-Festuniform für die Kapelle. Im Winter trägt man blaue Hosen. Auf diesem Waffenrock trägt man keine Ranginsignien.

C1 Diese Uniform ist so ähnlich wie die der Truppen und die Uniform im Zweiten Weltkrieg. **C2** Diese Uniform basiert auf einer australischen Uniform, die 1943 an die Erste Marinedivision in Australien ausgegeben wurde. **C3** Seit 1928, nach Einführung des offenen Kragens, hat sich diese '*Marine-green-*' Uniform mit Rankwinkeln von 1937 kaum geändert. Schulterbesätze der Einheit—hier die 6. Marinedivision—verschwanden 1947.

D1 Diese Sommeruniform wurde 1976 abgeschafft. Sie hatte sich sein 1928 kaum verändert. **D2** Die Truppen trugen auf ihrer Sommeruniform nur zwischen 1952 und 1961 Abzeichen auf dem Kragen. **D3** Die vollständige Khakiuniform wurde 1976 abgeschafft und durch diese Kombination ersetzt. Besondere Merkmale für Drill-Ausbilder ist der Hut mit breiter Krempe sowie die Degenkoppel.

E1 Diese Uniform wurde 1952 eingeführt. Der einzige Unterschied zwischen der Uniform für Offiziere und für Truppen sind die Rankinsignien. **E2** Diese Uniform trug man zwischen 1952 und 1969. **E3** Dies ist eine *Dress Blues*-Ausführung für weibliche Soldaten, allerdings ohne helleren Rock—man hielt die Ausführung in zwei Farbtönen bei Frauen für unvorteilhaft. Sie hat sich sein 1952 bis heute kaum geändert.

F1 '*Utilities*' aus dem Jahre 1944; der Rest der Kleidung stammt ebenfalls aus dem Zweiten Weltkrieg. **F2** Ein Maschinengewehrschütze mit eigener, automatischer Pistole. Diese Art von Ausrüstung bezeichnet man als *Light Marching Pack*. **F3** *HBT 'Utility'*-Uniform von 1942 mit Ausrüstung aus dem Zweiten Weltkrieg. Die Segeltuchgamaschen und die Helmtarnung waren 1950 für die Marine charakteristisch.

G1 Die Parka-Kaputze passte an und für sich über den Helm, aber man trug sie meistens so wie hier. Die Überschuhe aus Gummi und Segeltuch verursachten Kondensationsprobleme, der Schweiss innen gefrieren konnte. **G2** Feldjacke von 1943, die man warm gefüttert über einem Pullover trug. Der Soldat könnte, abgesehen von der pelzgefütterten Mütze, aus dem Zweiten Weltkrieg stammen. **G3** Die erste Panzerweste, die an amerikanische Truppen wurde, war die hier gezeigte, im Frühjahr 1952 ausgegebene Marineversion M1951. Die BAR-Gewehr erwies sich in Korea als nützlich; im Spezialgürtel trug man dafür 12 Magazine.

H1 Diese Spezial-Nachrichteneinheiten unterstanden direkt der *Fleet Marine Force Atlantic* und *Pacific*. Die Tarnuniform aus dem Zweiten Weltkrieg wurde für diese Fallschirm- und Unterwasser-spezialisten wider eingeführt. **H2** Die M1955-Panzerweste hatte unten Ösen, an denen man Ausrüstungsgegenstände befestigen konnte. Das ständige Herunterbaumeln dieser Gegenstände war so umständlich, dass wenige Männer von den Ösen Gebrauch machten. **H3** Die Mütze ist charakteristisch für die Marine seit dem Korea-Krieg; damals trug auch die Armee diese Mütze.

I1 Die Armee erwarb in Vietnam hergestellte Tarnuniformen mit tigerstreifen sowie vietnamesische Stiefel als Ersatz für die normalen '*Utility*'-Uniformen. Das Personal des *Recon Battalion* trug entweder schwarze oder gestreifte Mützen. Die Waffe ist ein Stoner 63, der von manchen Spezialeinheiten verwendet wurde. **I2** Die OG107 Armee-Kampfuniform, der M1961 Gürtel und das M-14 Gewehr waren typisch für die ersten Kriegsjahre in Vietnam. **I3** Dieser mit einem M-79-Granatenwerfer ausgerüstete Soldat trägt eine Gasmaske der Type M-17: sowohl die amerikanischen als auch die nordvietnamesischen Truppen verwendeten Gas im Einsatz. An den Socken sieht man, wie dürftig die Marine-Rationen waren. An das *Packboard* aus dem Zweiten Weltkrieg sind zwei Munitionskästen sowie persönliche Gegenstände geschnallt.

J1 Ab 1966 verwendete man Dschungel-'*Utilities*'. Die M1955-Panzerweste wurde mit Taschen versehen. Dieser Mann trägt ein M-60-Maschinengewehr, Munitionsgürtel und seine eigene Pistole. **J2** Ende 1968 beschloss man, für die gesamte Marine Tarnuniformen zu kaufen; es dauerte jedoch eine Weile, bis diese ausgegeben wurden. Nach Einführung der M-16-Gewehre kaufte man praktischerweise auch M1956-Patronentaschen. **J3** Der Pilot trägt einen feuerfesten CS/FRP-1-Overall und den SPH-3-Helm sowie die schwere Spezial-Panzerweste für Hubschraubercrews.

K1 Die neue Kevlar PASGT-Panzerweste, hier mit 'ALICE'-Ausrüstung und einem M203-Gewehr/Granatenwerfer. **K2** Dies ist die neue BDU-BDU-Kampfuniform-in 'Waldfarbe' mit LC-2-Ausrüstung. Die H&K MP-5 ist eine der beiden Waffen mit Schalldämpfer—die andere ist die Ingram, die von Marinespähtrupps verwendet wird. **K3** Seit Ende der 70er Jahre trägt die gesamte Marine Tarn-'*Utilities*'; da alte Lagerbestände aufgebraucht werden, sieht man sowohl 'Blattmuster' als auch 'Waldmuster'. Der Helm dieses Mannes, der zur DH-132-Panzerwagencrew gehört, ist passend zur Kleidung gestrichen.

L Marinepiloten trugen fast immer Kleidung und Ausrüstung der US Navy. Die Beschreibung hierzu in englischer Sprache erläutert jeden Artikel im einzelnen—diese Beschreibung lässt sich nicht genau übersetzen.